Quiet London

food & drink

Siobhan Wall

D1331891

FRANCES
LINCOLN

Quiet London: Food & Drink
© 2014 Quarto Publishing plc.
Text and photographs © Siobhan Wall 2014
Except photographs copyright © page 6 David Loftus; page 14, 21
Nicholas Haeffner; page 16 The Square, Mayfair; page 24 Simpson's in
the Strand; page 27 Orso; page 28 Lisa Barber; page 32 The Orangery;
page 39, 51, 96 Kirstin McKee; page 60 Stephanie Wolff Photography;
page 66 The Wolseley; page 113 The White Horse

Every care has been taken to trace copyright holders. Any we have
been unable to trace are invited to contact the publishers so that a full
acknowledgement may be given in subsequent editions

First Published in 2014 by Frances Lincoln,
an imprint of The Quarto Group.
The Old Brewery, 6 Blundell Street,
London N7 9BH, United Kingdom.
www.QuartoKnows.com

A catalogue record for this book is available from the British Library.

ISBN 978-0-7112-3558-8

Edited and designed by Jane Havell Associates
Printed and bound in China
9 8 7 6 5 4 3

FRONT COVER Ragged Canteen at Beaconsfield, Lambeth; BACK
COVER Cheeses, Muswell Hill; page 1: Pimlico Farmers' Market / Wild
Country Organics; page 2: Kew Farmers' Market / Love By Cake; page
6: The Wolseley; page 9: Le Deuxième

FSC® C104723

MIX
Paper from
responsible sources

Brimming with creative inspiration, how-to projects and useful information
to enrich your everyday life, Quarto Knows is a favourite destination for those
pursuing their interests and passions. Visit our site and dig deeper with our
books into your area of interest: Quarto Creates, Quarto Cooks, Quarto Homes,
Quarto Lives, Quarto Drives, Quarto Explores, Quarto Gifts, or Quarto Kids.

Quiet London

food & drink

Contents

Introduction

I started looking for tranquil cafés and restaurants around six years ago for *Quiet London*, the first illustrated guide to muzac-free locations to eat, drink, read, wander and browse in the capital. From the moment it was published, this small book was appreciated by many readers. I noticed that a few people not only bought the guide for themselves, but also for close friends. Instead of just giving them something to read, they were also saying, 'I am giving you some quiet time – implicit permission to find tranquil moments in your life.' This was very encouraging, and I was really pleased to learn that I wasn't the only person to appreciate and seek out quiet locations in this busy city.

Starting to do research for three new *Quiet London* books on Culture, Quiet Corners and Food & Drink, I realised that discovering calm, peaceful places was not just about avoiding city noise and anonymous crowds but also about finding beautiful, serene locations that would make people feel happy. I only shot photographs in the daytime, but I wanted to come back after dark for the 'Midnight Apothecary' in the pretty Brunel Museum garden, to drink blackberry martinis surrounded by sunflowers, nasturtiums and lavender. I was delighted to have the opportunity to write about other quiet places in London, not only because there were many restaurants and cafés that I couldn't include in the first book, but also because some new places opened, which suggests that the more crowded London gets, the more people really appreciate peaceful places to eat and drink. Music-free cafés that didn't exist a few years ago include the friendly Suzzle on Brick Lane and the Dalston Eastern Curve Garden. This informal Hackney café was created on the old Eastern Curve railway and is a great place to sit under a leafy bower drinking homemade lemonade with a slice of orange-and-almond cake. Where else in London can the tea maker pick lemon verbena leaves from the bushes near your seat to make your herbal infusion? The Dalston Curve Garden, in particular, demonstrates the precious enthusiasm and commitment of local people, who put considerable effort into creating intimate green spaces in densely packed urban areas.

Life in London is much more pleasurable than ten years ago, with street food and small catering businesses producing delicious hot dishes and tasty cakes to eat at home. Without any fuss or big announcements, London seems to be quietly benefiting from the concept of Slow Cities, an idea that evolved from the Slow Food movement. This Italian campaign seeks to improve the 'quality of fabric of life in . . . local areas, as well as good food and wine . . . the cherishing of local traditions, a belief in diversity as opposed to globalisation and sameness, resistance to the frenetic pace of everyday life'. Although they state that towns or cities with more than 50,000 residents can't ever be called a Slow City, it seems that small pockets of London are turning into their ideal village-like communities, where food still has a connection to the farmer and grower. Lamb's Conduit Street in Bloomsbury is one such example – not only can you shop at the People's Supermarket, which has an excellent traiteur at the rear, but also visit Caroline and Friends, a shop selling clothes and jewellery from suppliers the owner knows personally and has worked with for decades.

The number of farmers' markets has increased in the last few years, too, with some stunningly beautiful new sites. Perched on top of a hill with dramatic views of the city far below, Horniman Gardens Farmers' Market is held in one of the most spectacular locations in the capital. In the centre of London, Bloomsbury Farmers' market transforms empty Torrington Square into a colourful, lively place to find organic food, brought here by the very people who cultivate the runner beans and tomatoes you are about to buy. It is hard to deny that shopping here is a much more pleasant experience than pushing a trolley round an artificially lit supermarket where most items on the shelves are the same, day in day out. One place to try out delicious foods in a quiet location, with time to chat to the person who cooked the dishes, is the Lone Fisherman – his spicy Caribbean patties with hot pepper sauce can be found at the weekend at Merton Abbey Mills Market.

Another thing I learnt while researching *Food & Drink* was that ideas that we assume to be quite new have often been done before. In 1827 Isambard Kingdom Brunel organised the world's first formal dinner underground in his new tunnel beneath the Thames. Surrounded by candlelight, fifty guests enjoyed their feast accompanied by the Coldstream Guards' regimental band. Those intrepid participants were London's first pop-up diners, and they must have been delighted to emerge into daylight after relishing their subterranean meal.

So what has changed in the last few years since the first *Quiet London* book was published? There are so many interesting new places to buy groceries or sit down to eat. Small pockets of London have been transformed from drab, nondescript streets into interesting neighbourhoods. From the organic grocers on Broadway Market, a few minutes' walk from the Regent's Canal, to Calvert Avenue, previously undistinguished locales are now great places to visit, with attractive shops, cafés and pubs to meet up at with friends at the weekend. Unfortunately, many of these locations stream music or play the radio which makes the few shops and cafés that don't even more precious and rare. After discovering that many people, not just myself, prefer to eat and drink in quieter places, this book only includes locations that do not play background music. Some cafés and restaurants might get lively after dark as diners enjoy talking to their friends, but at least they won't have to shout above someone else's choice of jazz or funk. I am also happy to say that, despite some initial doubts, when I revisited the places I included in the previous *Quiet London* book, it was clear that the muzac-free shops, tearooms and brasseries don't get overcrowded and raucous. I think my readers tend to tread quietly wherever they go.

So, after getting up early to pick up some Spanish padrón peppers from Garcia, an amazing delicatessen in Portobello Road, and a rye loaf from Sally Clarke's round the corner, stop by for a green vegetable curry for lunch at Makan Malaysian café. After work, spend the evening with friends at the sophisticated Le Deuxième restaurant in Covent Garden and, on your way home, pick up a box of sweet yellow Indian barfi from Ambala. *Quiet London: Food & Drink* shows that it's not only possible but also very pleasurable to enjoy food from all over the world without ever having to listen to someone else's choice of ambient music.

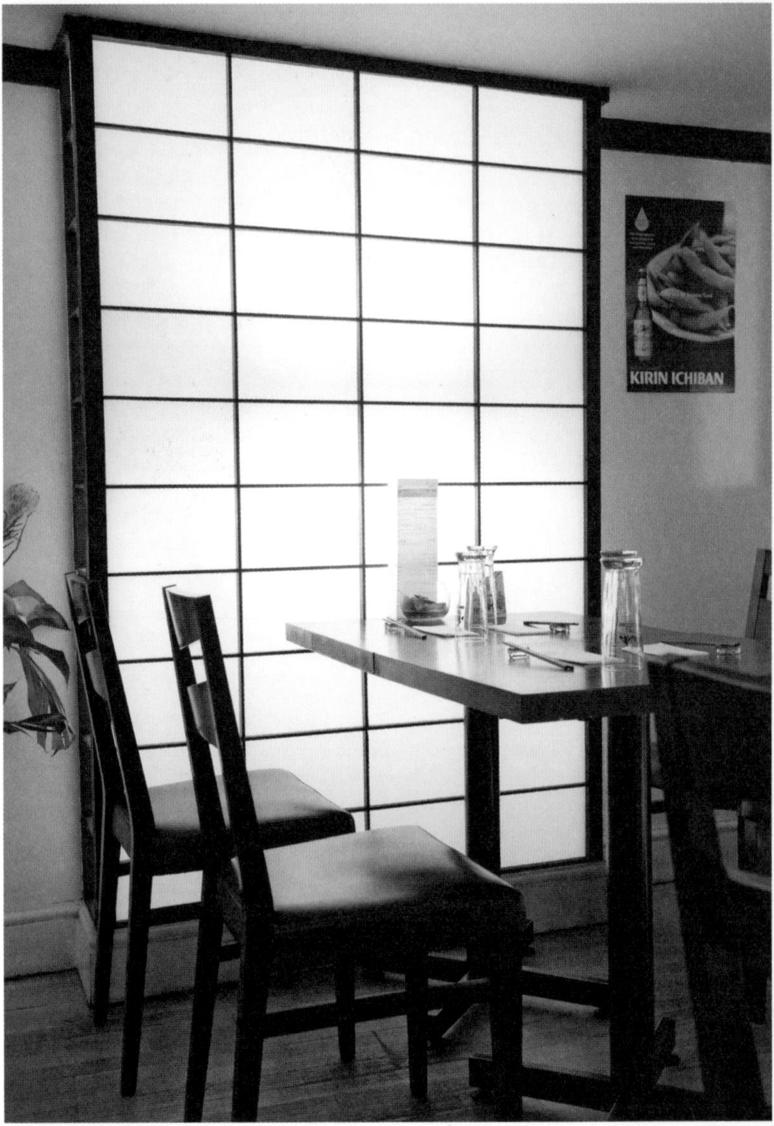
KIRIN ICHIBAN

Restaurants

Hazuki

43 Chandos Place, WC2N 4HS ☎ 020 7240 2530
www.hazukilondon.co.uk
Open lunch Monday–Friday 12–2.30pm, Saturday and Sunday 12.30–3pm; dinner Monday 6–10.30pm, Tuesday–Saturday 5–10.30pm, Sunday 5–9.30pm. Open during Easter and on New Year's Day
Tube Charing Cross, Leicester Square **Bus** 24, 29, 176
There is a 6cm step at the entrance and the toilets are down a flight of stairs

This small Japanese restaurant has been serving typical Eastern delicacies for many years. Their fish is freshly prepared by experienced sushi chefs who make sashimi platters for lovers of seafood. Also recommended are their set menus, where you can choose from assorted tempura, black cod miso, deep-fried oysters and delicious Teriyaki dishes. À la carte dishes include natto (fermented soybean) and grilled eel on rice. Finish your meal with a sweet sesame ice cream, and a few cups of gently warmed sake.

Como Lario

18–22 Holbein Place, SW1W 8NL ☎ 020 7730 2954
www.comolario.co.uk
Open Monday–Saturday 12.15–2.45pm, 6.30–11.30pm, Sunday 6.30–10pm,
closed Bank Holidays
Tube Sloane Square **Bus** 11, 137, 170, 211, 360, 452
There is a 4cm step at the entrance and the toilets are down a flight of stairs

With its white linen tablecloths and fresh flowers in china vases, this is a very
civilised place to have lunch or dinner. The black-and-white photos on the wall of
famous actors such as Marlene Dietrich and Marilyn Monroe are in keeping with
the sophisticated yet laid-back atmosphere. Como Lario serves mainly Northern
Italian dishes, and on the menu you might find carpaccio di salmone al limetta or
linguine sautéed with prawns, courgettes and saffron. Since 1969 they have been
experimenting with the classics, so as well as a mozzarella, cherry tomato and basil
salad you might find charcoal-grilled aubergines with Parma ham served with a
crusty bruschetta.

Le Deuxième

65 Long Acre, WC2E 9JD ☎ 020 7379 0033
www.ledeuxieme.com
Open Monday–Thursday 12–11pm, Friday and Saturday 12–11.30pm, Sunday 12–10pm, closed Bank Holidays
Tube Covent Garden **Bus** 24, 29, RV1
The restaurant is wheelchair accessible except for the toilet

This Covent Garden restaurant is an excellent place to come for a business lunch or a dinner with friends. With its beige leather seating and minimalist interior, the look of the restaurant is simple and understated. There are small white china vases of orchids on each immaculate table and a huge mauve crystal amethyst sits quietly in one corner. Situated close to the Royal Opera House, this stylish restaurant offers a pre-theatre menu and stays open late. The emphasis is on modern European dishes, such as pea and broadbean risotto, with main courses including confit of duck and desserts such as lemon tart. With over 150 wines to choose from on their extensive list, there will always be one to suit your palate.

Taste of Sichuan

167 High Street, Walthamstow, E17 7BX ☎ 020 3583 8864
www.tasteofsichuan.co.uk
Open Daily 11am–11pm
Tube Walthamstow Central **Bus** 58, 212, 230, 275, 675, W15
The restaurant is wheelchair accessible

From the outside, this unpretentious café looks like any other Chinese takeaway in
Walthamstow. It might serve fast food, but few people realise that Taste of Sichuan
dishes up some of the best Sichuan cuisine in the capital. Order smacked cucumber
and vegetable spring rolls to begin, followed by their excellent steamed sea bass with
spring onions. Their black bean seafood and spicy cumin beef on rice are not your
usual Chinese restaurant dishes, and are both tasty and filling. Come with a group of
friends and order a range of dishes to create your own unique banquet. You will leave
impressed with both the quality of the food and the reasonable bill.

Andrew Edmunds
46 Lexington Street, Soho W1F 0LW ☎ 020 7437 5708
www.andrewedmunds.com
Open Monday–Saturday 12–3.30pm (12.30–3.30pm Saturday), 5.30–10.45pm,
Sunday 1–4pm, 6–10.30pm but a few light dishes and drinks can be ordered
between these times **Tube** Leicester Square, Piccadilly **Bus** 14, 19, 38
The ground-floor tables are accessible but the toilets are down a flight of stairs

This is a very amenable, welcoming restaurant where nothing has changed in the last
twenty years. Andrew Edmunds has had a print shop next door for three decades and
many years ago decided to open a restaurant alongside his thriving business. Diners
say, 'Everything's perfect,' from the simple dressed crab to the wild sea bass fillet
with poppy seed potato cake, fennel and tomato salad and brown crab dressing. Ask
to see their extensive wine list, and sit with a full glass at one of the candlelit tables
by the window. It is advisable to book at least a day in advance, as locals know this is
a place to treasure.

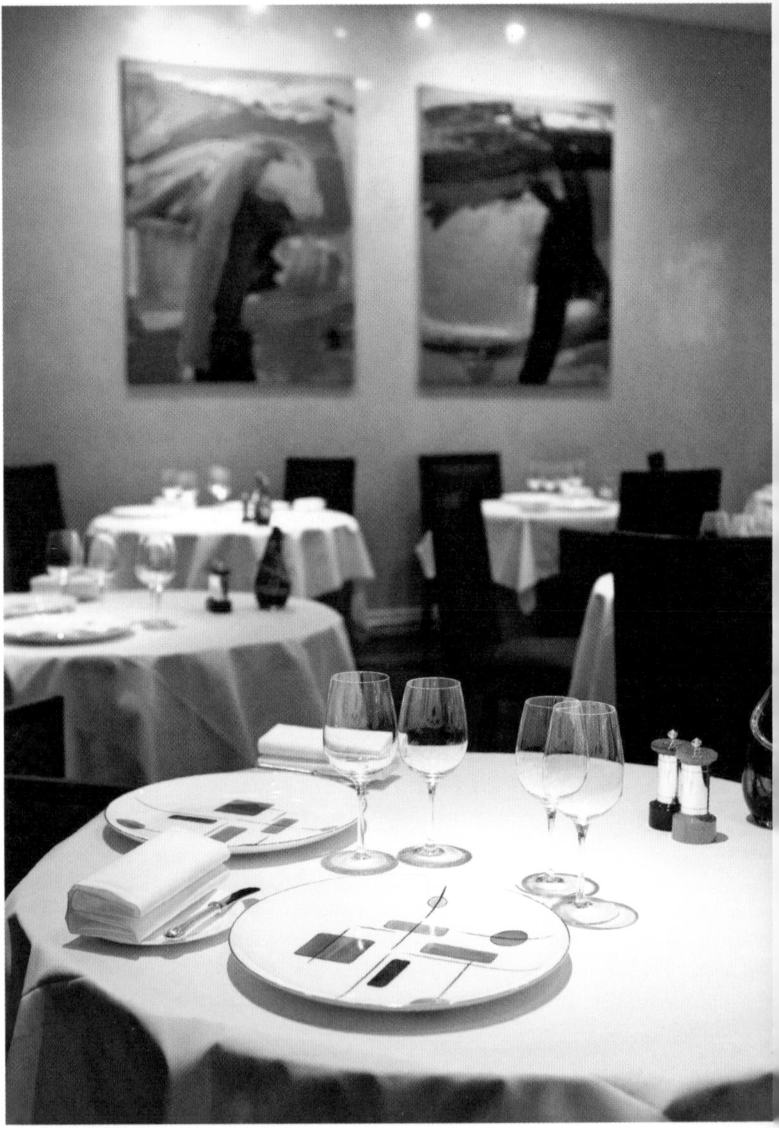

The Square, Mayfair
6–10 Bruton Street, W1J 6PU ☎ 020 7495 7100
www.squarerestaurant.com
Open Monday–Saturday 12–2.45pm, 6.30–10pm, Sunday 6.30–9.30pm
Tube Green Park, Bond Street **Bus** 2, 8, 10, 16, 19, 36, 38, 73, 74, 82, 137, 148, 414, 436
The restaurant is fully wheelchair accessible

Located between Green Park and Bond Street, this exclusive Mayfair restaurant is renowned for its fine dining and flawless service. Using seasonal ingredients, owner and chef Philip Howard's inventive menu reflects the huge variety of ingredients which can be sourced throughout the year. A typical lunchtime dish in this Michelin-starred restaurant might be roast quail breast with baked potatoes, roscoff onions, Vacherin Mont d'Or cheese and smoked bacon, followed by caramelised shoulder of suckling pig, sweet and sour orange, creamed potato and Tokyo turnips. Puddings tend to be just as appealing, with a moist rum baba with poached pineapple and chantilly crème tempting even the most resolute. À la carte and tasting menus are available both in the evening and at lunchtime, so for a special occasion it is worth coming here to enjoy some extraordinary cuisine.

Gauthier Soho

21 Romilly Street, W1D 5AF ☎ 020 7494 3111
www.gauthiersoho.co.uk
Open Monday 6.30–10.30pm, Tuesday–Saturday 12–2.30pm, 6.30–10.30pm,
Sunday 12–2.30pm
Tube Leicester Square, Tottenham Court Road **Bus** 14, 19, 24, 29, 38, 176
There are steps at the entrance and no wheelchair access to the toilets upstairs

As soon as you enter this beautifully proportioned Georgian townhouse, you feel
at ease. Diminutive chandeliers hang in the hallway and abstract paintings fill the
taupe-hued walls. In the ground-floor dining room, soft grey carpets and ornate
carved fireplaces create a calm ambience. Alexis Gauthier's modern French cuisine is
quite a draw for Soho diners who adore his outstanding dishes. Book well in advance
to try the goût du jour – perhaps black winter truffle with acquarello riso, wild Cornish
sea bass with black olive paté and spinach gnocchi – and end the evening with his
extraordinary 'Louis XV' nut and chocolate dessert.

St John

26 St John Street, EC1M 4AY ☎ 020 7251 0848 www.stjohnrestaurant.com
Open Monday–Friday bar 11am–11pm, restaurant 12–3pm, 6–11pm, Saturday bar and restaurant 6–11pm, Sunday bar 12–5pm, restaurant 1–3pm, closed Bank Holidays
Tube Barbican, Farringdon **Bus** 17, 45, 46, 55, 63, 243
There is disabled access to the bar and conservatory dining area, but not the first-floor restaurant. The use of mobile phones is not permitted in the dining room

The high-ceilinged white rooms of this bakery, bar and restaurant used to be a meat smokery for nearby Smithfield Market, and you can still look up into the huge tower where gammon and pork were hung and cured until the late 1960s. As well as having a great bakery, selling rye loaves, seed cakes and soda bread, the restaurant serves flavoursome food in season, so the menu changes throughout the year. In the autumn, try their woodcock or grilled ox heart with rape greens and mustard, followed by an apple sorbet with Polish vodka. St John stocks only French wine direct from the producers and their Minervois comes from their own winery. The food is superlative yet the restaurant has a laid-back, relaxed informality which encourages a slow appreciation of the culinary pleasures to be had here.

Elena's L'Etoile

30 Charlotte Street, Fitzrovia W1T 2NG ☎ 020 7636 7189
www.elenasletoile.co.uk
Open Monday–Friday 12–2.45pm, 6–10.30pm, Saturday 6–10.30pm, closed Sunday and
Bank Holidays **Tube** Goodge Street **Bus** 10, 14, 24, 29, 73, 134, 390
There is a 20cm step at the entrance, making it difficult for wheelchair users to gain
access

Having celebrated its centenary around twenty years ago, this comfortable yet
glamorous French-style bistro is a great place to enjoy good conversation over a
three-course meal. With its red plush chairs, white table linen and large mirrors
surrounded by photo portraits of famous actors and celebrities, this is a place to see
and be seen. Named after Elena Salvoni, who was maître d' here until well into her
nineties, L'Étoile serves mainly French dishes with a modern twist. A typical soup
might be butternut squash with St Maure's goats' cheese, crostini and almond flakes,
followed by a main course of roasted lamb rump with aubergine, red peppers and
spinach and rosemary jus.

Husk

649-651 Commercial Road, E14 7LW ☎ 020 7702 8802
www.huskcoffee.com/coffee
Open Monday 9am–6pm, Tuesday–Friday 8am–9pm, Saturday 10am–5pm, closed
Sundays and most Bank Holidays
DLR Limehouse **Bus** 15, 115,135, D3
The café is wheelchair accessible

This large, friendly café is one of the nicest places to meet friends for coffee in East
London. Run by a Christian organisation, the staff are welcoming, and fair trade
products are much more visible than any evangelical leaflets. Although ambient
music is played, if you come to here to read a book in one of their vintage chairs, you
won't notice the background chatter. You'll find all sorts of people here, from parents
with babies in pushchairs to local office workers dropping by for a spicy dhal with
naan bread on their lunch break. Alongside serving great coffee, Husk organises
fitness classes (try 'One Body, One Soul, One Spirit on Saturdays) and the Tearfund
runs storytelling sessions, encouraging local Bangladeshi, Somalian and Moroccan
families to share their traditional tales.

Wild Honey Restaurant

12 St George Street, W1S 2FB ☎ 020 7758 9160
www.wildhoneyrestaurant.co.uk
Open Monday–Saturday 12–2.30pm, 6–10.30pm, closed Bank Holidays
Tube Oxford Circus **Bus** 6, 10, 23, 55, 73, 88, 98, 139, 159, 453, C2
The ground-floor tables are wheelchair accessible but not the toilets in the basement

The look of this beautiful dining room is enough to tempt any diner to linger here
for an evening of culinary delights. The contemporary artworks on the walls are
entrancing and the mustard- and peach-coloured velvet dining chairs are as
comfortable to sit on as they are attractive to the eye. The English/Asian/French-
inspired menu changes daily and reflects the seasons throughout the year. The
chef at Wild Honey worked with Bruno Loubet for a while, and his octopus carpaccio
and morello cherry lemonade are well worth a visit to this lovely restaurant.
Other inventive dishes include Scottish scallops with flourless gnocchi, Dover sole
with red quinoa and brussels sprouts and partridge with damson jam and green
freekah wheat.

Rules Restaurant

35 Maiden Lane, Covent Garden WC2E 7LB ☎ 020 7836 5314
www.rules.co.uk
Open Daily 12pm–12am, closed Christmas Day and Boxing Day
Tube Covent Garden, Leicester Square **Bus** 1, 168, 176, 188, 243
The ground-floor wheelchair access is good but the toilets are on the first floor

Rules first opened its doors in 1798 as an oyster bar, making it the oldest restaurant in London. The entire building has a tangible sense of history and many famous people have dined here, including Charles Dickens, Laurence Olivier, Charlie Chaplin, Ava Gardner and a few currently serving politicians. Edward VII used to arrive with a friend by a secret entrance and it is no wonder he appreciated coming here. The listed building is sumptuously decorated, with hunting trophies, antique prints, silver cutlery and red wax candles on starched white linen. Specialising in classic game cookery, the venison and wild birds served here are all sourced from the Lartington Estate, with occasional beef from their grass-fed Galloway herd in the Pennines.

Simpson's in the Strand

100 The Strand, WC2R 0EW ☎ 020 7836 9112
www.simpsonsinthestrand.co.uk
Open Monday–Friday 12–2.45pm and 5.45–10.30pm, Saturday 12–2.45pm and
5–10.30pm, Sunday 12–9pm
Tube Charing Cross, Covent Garden **Bus** 6, 9, 11, 13, 15, 23, 87, 91, 139, 176
The restaurant and bar are wheelchair accessible

For over 170 years the historic Simpson's in the Strand has been offering classic
British dishes to Londoners and visitors to the capital. Many famous writers and
artists have dined here, from Vincent Van Gogh and Charles Dickens to George
Bernard Shaw. Simpson's originally opened in 1828 as a chess club and coffee house;
to avoid disturbing the chess games in progress, large joints of meat were placed on
silver-domed trolleys and wheeled to guests' tables for carving – a practice Simpson's
still continues today. For a convivial lunch, order a smoked haddock omelette, their
classic beef wellington and finish your hearty meal with a traditional treacle pudding.

Dosa World

46 Hanbury Street, E1 5JL ☎ 020 7377 0344
www.dosa-world.com
Open Tuesday–Thursday 11.30am–3pm and 5–11pm, Friday–Saturday 11.30am–3pm
and 5–11.30pm, Sunday 12–10pm
Tube Aldgate East **Train** Shoreditch High Street **Bus** 25, 67
The restaurant is wheelchair accessible

This small restaurant is the only one around Brick Lane which serves South Indian
food, including the delicious crispy rice and lentil pancakes called dosas. Although
they play background music, there are only 16 seats so if you bring a few friends they
will gladly turn the sound system off. The staff are very helpful and considerate, and
this low-key restaurant feels informal and intimate. Try their vegetarian thali – an
entire meal in itself, with spicy sambal, rice and a lentil-and-vegetable curry, all
served in small stainless steel dishes on a tray. Their speciality is cabbage thoran
served with crunchy mixed pickle and a cooling carrot-and-cucumber raita, a rare
treat for lovers of South Indian cuisine.

Orso

27 Wellington Street, WC2E 7DB ☎ 020 7240 5269
www.orsorestaurant.co.uk
Open Monday–Saturday 12pm–12am, Sunday 12–9pm
Tube Temple, Covent Garden **Bus** 6, 9, 11, 13, 15, 23, 87, 91, 139, 176
The restaurant is not wheelchair accessible

This well-established Italian restaurant used to be an orchid warehouse, where
blooms for the Covent Garden flower market were stored deep underground. Since
1985 Orso has been serving authentic Italian cuisine to opera-goers and lovers
of fine food. The set pre-theatre menu offers three choices, including a salad of
goat's cheese, radish, lambs' lettuce, fennel and endive with fig balsamic dressing,
delicious pan-fried mackerel with crushed new potato, spinach and salsa verde and
a slice of their delectable lemon cake with blueberry compote. They are renowned
for their extensive list of imaginative cocktails so, after a visit to the ballet, slowly sip
their Espresso Martini – a luscious mix of espresso coffee, Stolichnaya vodka and
Crème de Cacao.

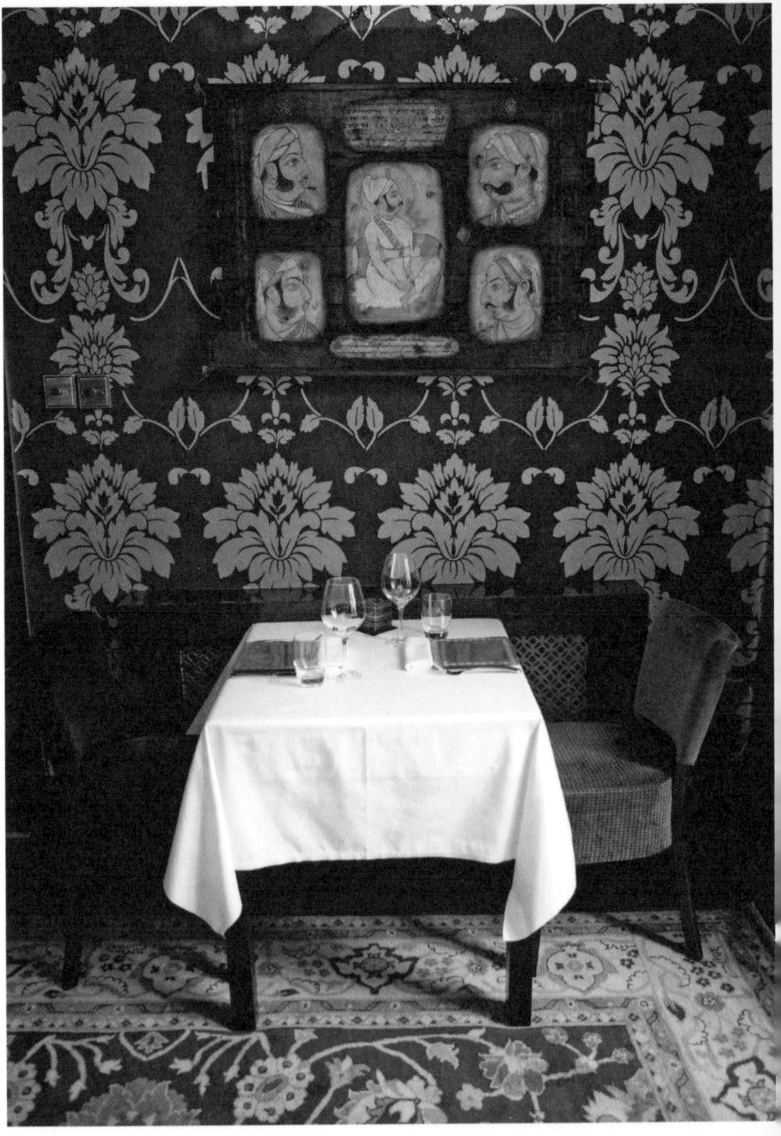

Rasoi

10 Lincoln Street, Chelsea SW3 2TS ☎ 020 7225 5181
www.mandarinoriental.com/geneva/fine-dining/rasoi-by-vineet
Open Tuesday–Saturday 12–2pm and 7–10pm, closed over major holidays (check website for details)
Tube Sloane Square **Bus** 19, 22
There are steps into the restaurant but wheelchair users can be accommodated

Rasoi means 'kitchen' and this sophisticated Indian restaurant serves up delicious South Asian dishes in a beautiful 100-year-old townhouse. The walls are decorated in warm, ornate patterns and the judicious arrangement of carvings, silks and Indian trinkets adds to the comfortable ambience. Considered one of the best Indian restaurants in Britain, this Michelin-starred venue is a rather special place to dine. The menu is consistently innovative yet draws on traditional Indian cuisine. Typical dishes on the seven-course tasting menu might be banana-wrapped mustard tilapia with aubergine achari couscous, mango-tellicherry pepper chicken and their delicate champagne-rose petal sorbet sweetened with rose marmalade.

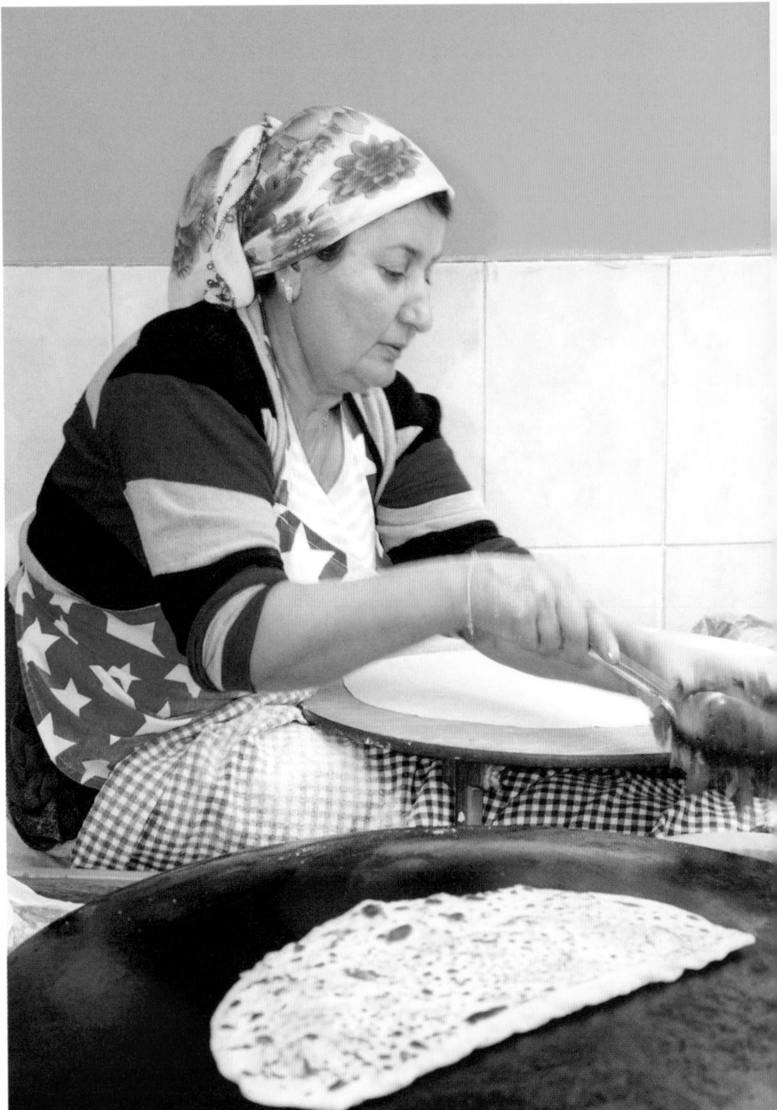

Cafés & places for afternoon tea

Basak Pastenesi

7 Newington Green, Stoke Newington N16 9PX ☎ 020 7359 2338
Open Daily 7.30am–7pm, including Christmas Day
Train Canonbury, Dalston Kingsland **Bus** 30, 73, 141, 236, 243, 341, 476
The shop and café are wheelchair accessible

This may be the only bakery in London where you can see your durum bread being rolled out and baked on a hot griddle in the window. Even though you are in North London, the friendly women who work here make this small café and patisserie feel as if you have arrived in a Turkish village. On a summer day, take your piping hot, delicious lahmacun (Turkish pizza), zeytinli (olive) bread, some pistachio baklava and a few beakers of ayran yoghurt drink for a Mediterranean picnic on Newington Green.

The Orangery

Kensington Palace, Kensington Gardens, W8 4PX ☎ 020 3166 6113
www.orangerykensingtonpalace.co.uk
Open Daily 10–11.30am, 12–6pm
Private events are often held at The Orangery, check website for closures
Tube High Street Kensington, Queensway **Bus** 9, 10, 49, 52, 70, 94, 148, 390, 452
Wheelchair access is via a ramp which is situated on the right side of the terrace

Built as a pavilion for Queen Anne in 1704, these graceful rooms have been
transformed into a sunlit café overlooking Kensington Palace's immaculately kept
gardens. This is a very civilised place to sit on the outdoor terrace on sunny days
underneath a white parasol. The lunch menu suggests free range egg-and-cress
sandwiches, leek-and-potato soup and fish stew, while the famous Orangery
afternoon tea includes Duchess of Bedfordshire cake, old English jam tart and ten
speciality teas. Enjoy your orange posset with a glass of fine wine, knowing that
anyone can now sit in this elegant room designed for a Hanoverian queen.

The Cloister Café Great St Bartholomew's

West Smithfield, EC1A 9DS ☎ 020 7600 0440
www.greatstbarts.com/Pages/Cloister_Cafe/cafe.html
Open Monday–Friday 8.30am–4pm, Sunday 9.30am–1:30pm, 5–6pm for afternoon tea
until Evensong begins, closed Saturday **Tube** Barbican, Farringdon, St Paul's
Bus 4, 8, 17, 25, 45, 46, 56, 63, 100, 153, 242, 243, 341, 521
There is step-free access to the church and café along the path leading to the West
Door but no wheelchair access to the outside toilets

Enter the beautiful Great St Bartholomew's Church by passing underneath the
Elizabethan gatehouse. After slowly wandering round its hallowed interior, find a
table in this tranquil café to the right of the main porch. There aren't many places
where you can sit and have a slice of chocolate cake among fifteenth-century
cloisters, but the ancient surroundings make this one of the nicest cafés in London
to enjoy afternoon tea. Fresh mint tea is served in white china pots, and with the pale
green light filtering through the leaded glass windows this is one of the most peaceful
corners in England.

The Brunel Museum Café

Railway Avenue, Rotherhithe SE16 4LF
☎ 020 7231 3840
www.brunel-museum.org.uk
Open Daily 10am–5pm, late opening
Thursday
Train Rotherhithe
Bus 1, 188, 381, C10
The café is wheelchair accessible

This little-known museum shows the
history of Sir Marc Isambard Brunel's
Engine House, and one corner has been
converted into a small café. Have a cup
of tea surrounded by drawings produced
by local artists on the curved walls.

Dalston Eastern Curve Garden

13 Dalston Lane, Hackney E8 3DF
www.dalstongarden.org
Open Daily 11am–6pm, café 11am–7pm
and later for evening events
Train Dalston Junction, Dalston
Kingsland **Bus** 30, 38, 76, 149, 236, 242,
243, 277, 488
The garden, café and toilets are
wheelchair accessible

Enjoy a peppermint tea and a freshly
baked banana cake in this relaxing café
overlooking a pretty garden. The outdoor
benches are a delightful place to sit on
summer afternoons. Stay late for an
artisanal beer or a pizza baked in their
outdoor clay oven.

Crêperie Cafe

127 Church Road, Barnes SW13 9HR
Open Daily 8am–5pm (winter), 8am–8pm (summer)
Tube Hammersmith **Train** Barnes, Barnes Bridge
Bus 22, 33, 209, 265, 283, 337, 419, 485
The café is wheelchair accessible

With its ornate mirrors and glass chandeliers, this pretty café in Barnes Village has a relaxing French ambience. The chef used to work at La Durée in Paris so is an expert patissier, but you can also order one of his freshly made crêpes, a slice of home-made carrot cake or a croque-monsieur. For lunch, enjoy salad with potato tortilla followed by a nougat stick for dessert – a sweet which could be described as a mini-Danish pastry covered in chocolate and almonds. The café also serves freshly squeezed carrot juice, thick fruit smoothies and a wide range of teas, including jasmine pearls and a soothing liquorice-peppermint mix.

Gaby's Deli

30 Charing Cross Road, WC2H 0DE ☎ 020 7836 4233
Open Monday–Saturday 9am–midnight, Sunday 11am–10pm
Tube Leicester Square, Charing Cross **Bus** 14, 19, 24, 29, 38, 176
There is wheelchair access but the entrance is narrow

The longevity of this popular deli restaurant comes as no surprise. Located near the major art museums around Trafalgar Square, Gaby and his staff have been serving up salt beef sandwiches, hot chickpea falafels and crunchy salads for five decades now. Whether you are here for a substantial lunch or a quick bite on the way to the theatre, it's a real pleasure to choose from the dishes on the counter and pile your plate high with colourful vegetables, creamy hummus and a smoked salmon bagel. The café has a licence, so you can order a glass of house red or white to accompany your meal in this unpretentious Middle Eastern deli.

Makan Café

270 Portobello Road, W10 5TY ☎ 020 8960 5169
www.makancafe.co.uk
Open Daily 9am–9.30pm
Tube Ladbroke Grove, Westbourne Park **Bus** 28, 52, 70, 295, 452
There is an 8cm step at the entrance

The chefs start chopping and slicing early in the morning, so a few dishes will be
ready by the time you arrive for a cooked halal breakfast. Makan is famous for the
owner's very own Malaysian green curry recipe, made with chillis and lemongrass,
but you can also try her Singaporean laksa, Indonesian mee goreng and spicy Indian
dhal. Everything is cooked fresh daily and available from the counter, so you can also
take home a variety of delicious vegetarian and meat dishes. If you don't have time for
a tasty South East Asian meal, you can drop in for a coffee and a slice of their coconut
and banana cakes.

Handmade Food

40 Tranquil Vale, Blackheath SE3 0BD ☎ 0208 297 9966
www.handmadefood.com
Open Tuesday–Saturday 9am–10pm, Sunday 9am–5pm, closed Monday and Bank
Holidays **Train** Blackheath **Bus** 89, 108, 202, 386
The café is wheelchair accessible and has a ground-floor table

Every day the menu changes at this award-winning traiteur and café, and wondering
what will emerge from the kitchen is part of the pleasure of coming here. Whether you
take away their dish of the day or eat here, you won't be disappointed with the textures
and flavours of the delicious food. Try the Moroccan-style chicken pastilla served
with cumin yoghurt and türlü (Turkish vegetable stew) or their cauliflower, leek and
celeriac gratin. Ethically sourced and sustainable food tends to be prepared with care
and inventiveness, and Handmade Food is a great example of how to do this well.

German Deli Warehouse Shop

Unit 1, The Hamlet Industrial Estate, 96 White Post Lane, Hackney Wick E9 5EN
☎ 020 8985 5385 www.germandeli.co.uk
Open Tuesday–Friday 11am–7pm, Saturday–Monday 11am–5pm
Train Hackney Wick **Bus** 108, 276, 308, 588
The ground floor is wheelchair accessible with a 4cm step to the toilets

It is hard to decide whether to call the German Deli a shop or a café – it is both, of course, and this unusual venue is located in the middle of industrial Hackney Wick. Many of the surrounding buildings now house small businesses and art galleries, so the German Deli has a varied clientele. Try their bratwurst and sauerkraut sandwiches or a slice of lemon cheesecake with a pot of limeflower tea. The partitioned spaces upstairs are as eclectic as the diners – a typical Bavarian room has a cuckoo clock on the wall while the balcony has views over an intriguing garden shed and outdoor patio. Don't be put off by the location – the staff are friendly and the atmosphere unpretentious but upbeat. This is a good place to hang out with up-and-coming artists.

The Angel Inn

420 St John Street, EC1V 4NJ ☎ 020 7837 7946
Open Monday–Friday 6.30am–4pm, Saturday 6.30am–3pm, Sunday 9am–3pm, closed
Christmas Day, Boxing Day and New Year's Day
Tube Angel **Bus** 19, 38, 153, 274, 341
The café is wheelchair accessible

This is a greasy spoon with a menu to suit everyone, from city gent to builder's
mate. Drop in for a huge weekday cooked breakfast with baked beans on toast and
fried eggs, then bring your children at the weekend for knickerbocker glories and
milkshakes. The chefs also cook substantial lunches at very reasonable prices,
including roast chicken with potatoes and vegetables or fish and chips followed by
roly-poly pudding with custard. On a Sunday you could even bring your aunt for an
Americano coffee and Danish pastry after a trip to the local antique markets.

Patisserie Valerie

15 Bedford Street, Covent Garden WC2 9HE ☎ 020 7379 6428
www.patisserievalerie.co.uk
Open Monday–Friday 7.30am–9pm, Saturday 8.30am–9pm, Sunday 9am–8pm
Tube Covent Garden, Leicester Square **Bus** 6, 9, 11, 13, 15, 23, 87, 91, 139, 176
The café is wheelchair accessible

Madame Valerie came to London from Belgium and opened her first patisserie in
Frith Street, Soho, in 1926. After the premises were bombed in the Second World War,
she moved to Old Compton Street where her teashop can still be found today. None
of the Patisserie Valerie cafés play background music, but the popularity of their
delicious cakes and pastries does mean they can be quite lively. The Covent Garden
branch tends to be quieter, although if you want a really peaceful afternoon tea, you
can book the private upstairs room in Soho for yourself and a few quiet friends.

Sable d'Or

249 Muswell Hill Broadway, N10 1DE ☎ 020 8442 1330
www.sabledor.co.uk
Open Monday–Friday 7.30am–6pm, Saturday and Sunday 7.30am–6.30pm,
closed Christmas Day **Tube** East Finchley, Bounds Green **Bus** 43, 102, 134, 234
There is a small step at the entrance

The title of this pleasant café translates as 'Golden Sand', and the elegant French
chandeliers and North African tiles suggest a Mediterranean influence. Drop in
for a croissant and coffee for breakfast, then come back for a lemon, frangipani or
pear apricot tart around 11am. If you have time, discuss the issues of the day over
a sun-dried tomato, mozzarella and olive ciabatta sandwich for lunch. Delicious
viennoisseries can be bought at the counter to take home or enjoyed with a cup of
tea in this stylish café. Artists show their work here in monthly changing exhibitions,
which means that if you run out of conversation you can always discuss the paintings
on the walls.

Manze Eel and Pie House

87 Tower Bridge Road, SE1 4TW ☎ 020 7277 6181
www.manze.co.uk
Open Monday 11am–2pm, Tuesday–Thursday 10.30am–2pm, Friday 10am–2.30pm,
Saturday 10am–2.45pm
Tube Borough, Bermondsey **Bus** 42, 78, 188
Manze is wheelchair accessible

Manze's started baking pies in 1892 and is the oldest pie and mash shop still standing.
Michele Manze, the original owner's son-in-law, bought the premises in 1902 and,
amazingly, the café still has its original marble tables, wooden benches, green and
white wall tiles and pristine shop fittings. The Manzes came from Italy, and initially
sold ice creams in the premises next door until they bought the shop. Michele's
grandsons now run the shop and café, keeping their secret liquor recipe in the family.
Here you can pick up some chilled jellied eels or a hot meat or vegetarian pie, baked
fresh every day on the premises. Sit down and reminisce about the area with a beef
and gravy pie, a glass of something sweet and fizzy and a plate of hot stewed eels.

Quaker Centre Café

Friends House, 173–177 Euston Road, NW1 2BJ ☎ 020 7663 1000
www.friendshouse.co.uk/cafe
Open Monday–Friday 8am–8pm, Saturday 8am–3.30pm, closed Sundays and
Bank Holidays
Tube Euston, Euston Square **Bus** 10, 18, 30, 73, 168, 205, 253, 390
The café is fully wheelchair accessible

The Quaker Centre Café can be found in a large room inside Friends' House on the
northern edge of Bloomsbury. The space was refurbished a few years ago, and the
1927 listed building is now a welcoming place to drop in and browse books or just
have a coffee and cake. The chill cabinets at the rear have apple, pear and beetroot
juices and vegetarian sandwiches while Danish pastries and cinnamon swirls can
be bought from the main counter. On sunny days you can take your herbal tea and
blueberry muffin to the inner courtyard and sit under a parasol. A restaurant in the
basement is open Monday–Friday 12–2pm if you prefer a more substantial lunch.

Jewish Museum Café

129–131 Albert Street, Camden NW1 7NB ☎ 020 7284 7384
www.jewishmuseum.org.uk/cafe
Open Sunday–Thursday 10am–5pm, Friday 10am–2pm, museum open on Bank
Holidays but closed for Jewish festivals, Christmas Day and Boxing Day
Tube Camden Town **Bus** 24, 27, 29, 31, 88, 134, 168, 214, 253, 274, C2
The museum and café are wheelchair accessible

The small kosher café in this beautifully designed museum is a good place to rest
your legs after visiting the precious Jewish artefacts and temporary exhibitions on the
other floors. Surrounded by pale wood panelling, the café has a modern, bright feel.
The kitchen is licensed by the Sephardi Kashrut Authority and offers freshly baked
cakes and pastries from a kosher bakery in Finchley. For lunch, their soup of the
day is a good option followed by a slice of apple strudel or honey cake with a cup
of herbal tea.

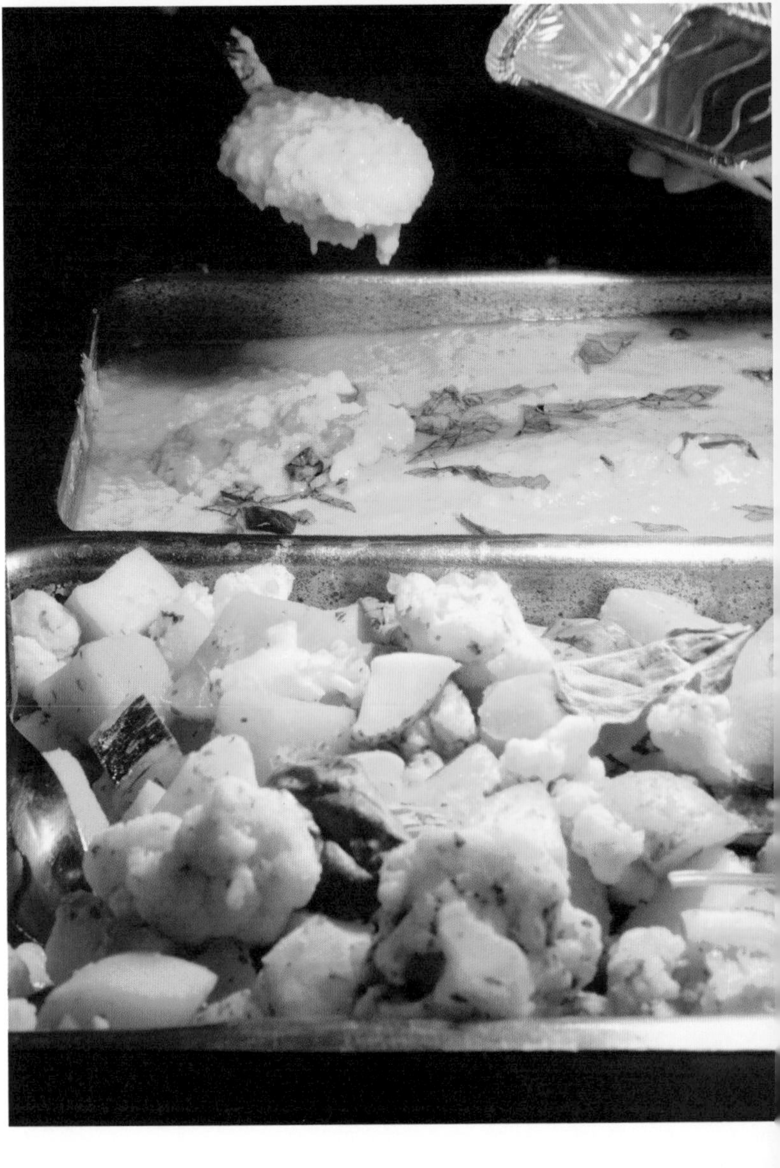

The Grain Shop

269a Portobello Road, W11 1LR ☎ 020 7229 5571
Open Monday–Saturday 10am–6pm, Sunday 10am–5pm, New Year's Day and during
the Notting Hill carnival
Tube Ladbroke Grove **Bus** 7, 23, 31, 70, 228
There is one small step but staff can serve customers at the door

If you ever feel tempted by delicious vegetarian dishes, this is the ideal place to pick
up a hot meal from the counter. The only problem is that there are so many enticing
stews and casseroles, it's always difficult to choose what to eat. The only way to solve
this is to come back again and again, but the dishes are changed regularly so you may
never get to try them all. The lentil and coconut dhal and the cauliflower and broccoli
bake are just two of their tempting seasonal meals. Although it is a take-away, you
can eat the Grain Shop's food in the MauMau café next door, as long as you buy a
drink there to go with your meal. Or invite your friends round for a gargantuan feast
and then pick up a chickpea curry, some stir-fried Thai vegetables and a few of their
delicious cakes.

Mary Ward Café

42 Queen Square, WC1N 3AQ ☎ 020 7269 6085
www.marywardcentre.ac.uk/about/cafe
Open During term time only Monday–Thursday 9.30am–8.45pm, Friday 9.30am–8pm,
Saturday 9.30am–4pm, closed Sunday; during summer school from 11–29 July
weekdays 9.30am–4.30pm
Tube Russell Square, Holborn **Bus** 38, 55, 59, 68, 91, 168, 243, 521
The café is fully wheelchair accessible and open to everyone

The Mary Ward Centre is celebrated for its adult education courses – from
archaeology to ukulele, Pilates to poetry, there are many ways to enlighten and
energise yourself here. After your class, make your way to the ground-floor
vegetarian café in this Grade II-listed Georgian building in pretty Queen Square.
The spicy cauliflower soup is nice and thick and, like everything else behind the
counter, the portions are generous. Side salads are piled high with grated carrot,
beetroot, beansprouts, radishes, cucumber, oak leaf lettuce and a choice of delicious
dressings. From tortillas to casseroles, everything is very reasonably priced, making
this is a great place to enjoy some incredible, freshly prepared food.

The Savannah at The Wesley

81–103 Euston Street, NW1 2EZ ☎ 020 7691 8588
www.thesavannah.co.uk
Open Restaurant daily 5–10pm, Bar Monday–Friday 11am–11pm, Saturday and
Sunday 12–11pm
Tube Euston, Warren Street **Bus** 30, 59, 73, 205
The restaurant is wheelchair accessible

Close to Euston Station but located down a quiet backstreet, this sustainable bar
and restaurant in the welcoming Wesley Hotel is a great place to visit either alone or
with friends. Artists have embellished the slate grey walls of the chic interior, adding
character to a calm and private space. You can either order a pot of tea and enjoy a
cake, or opt for a light lunch cooked with ethically sourced ingredients. Try their wild
mushroom and spinach risotto, with a side salad of rocket leaves and parmesan,
accompanied by a glass of organic wine or a craft beer. Follow this with one of
their delicious desserts, such as the chocolate olive oil mousse or the lemon basil
panacotta. All profits from the restaurant go to an educational charity, so you can
enjoy great food as well as knowing that your visit benefits others.

Future and Found

225A Brecknock Road, N19 5AA
☎ 020 7267 4772 www.futureandfound.com
Open Tuesday–Friday 10am–6.30pm,
Saturday 10am–6pm, Sunday 12am–6pm
Tube Tufnell Park **Bus** 4, 134, 390
There is a step at the entrance to the
shop but the café is fully accessible

In warm weather this pretty courtyard
becomes a delightful café tucked in-
between a typical London terrace and a
wonderful interior design shop. Future
and Found play background music
indoors, but you can take a seat outside
where it is quiet. Order some green tea
and homemade cake; soon brought out
to you by the friendly shop owners.

Paul Rothe & Son Delicatessen

35 Marylebone Lane, W1U 2NN
☎ 020 7935 6783
www.paulrotheandsondelicatessen.co.uk
Open Monday–Friday 8am–6pm,
Saturday 11am–5pm, closed Sunday
Tube Bond Street **Bus** 7, 10, 23, 18, 27,
30, 55, 73, 98, 159, C2
Small step at the entrance, several
steps down to customer toilet

This popular German deli has been
here since 1900, and customers come
back often for their gherkin and cream
cheese rolls and sliced meats. They
open early, so for breakfast you can
quietly read the morning paper while
enjoying a bacon sandwich and coffee.

Sotheby's Café

34–35 New Bond Street, W1A 2AA ☎ 020 7293 5821
www.sothebys.com/cafe
Open Daily 9.30–11.30am, 12–2.45pm, 3–4.45pm, closed at the weekend and on
Bank Holidays
Tube Oxford Circus, Bond Street, Green Park **Bus** 8
The café is fully wheelchair accessible

Located in the heart of Sotheby's Auction House, this beautiful café is a very tranquil
place to dine alone or with friends. With its large mirrored walls, white table linen
and black-and-white framed photography on the walls, this is a glamorous yet
comfortable place to have breakfast, lunch or afternoon tea. Classics such as Welsh
rarebit, Dumfries smoked salmon bagels and toasted tea cakes can all be ordered
from the tea menu. The only London auction house with its own café, you don't have
to attend a sale here to appreciate good food in a sophisticated atmosphere. The staff
are very warm and welcoming and, for a rather special lunch, order their lobster club
sandwich and treat yourself to a glass of champagne.

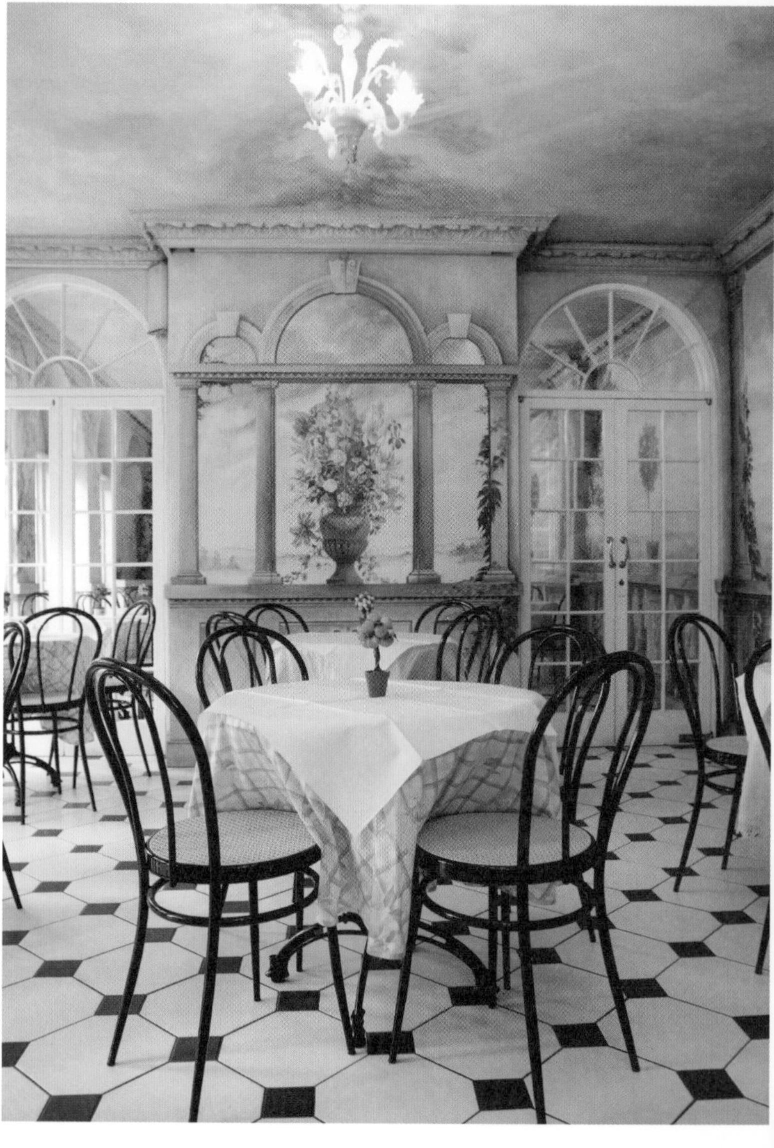

The Fan Orangery

The Fan Museum, 12 Crooms Hill, Greenwich SE10 8ER ☎ 020 8305 1441
£ Museum entry required, free to senior citizens and people with disabilities on Tuesday afternoon
www.thefanmuseum.org.uk/orangery
Open Tuesday and Sunday for afternoon tea, sittings at 1.45pm, 2.15pm, 3.15pm, 3.45 (advance booking required)
DLR Cutty Sark, Greenwich **Bus** 129, 177, 188, 199, 286, 386
The café and museum are wheelchair accessible

This delightful museum not only has over 4,500 fans in its specialist collection, it also has a small tearoom overlooking the fan-shaped parterre in the garden. The romantic trompe l'oeil mural on the orangery walls is the perfect surrounding for a very reasonably priced afternoon tea. This comes complete with scones, clotted cream and jam, freshly baked cakes and a pot of tea or coffee. It is hard to know how to enhance this charming setting, except by inviting your most appreciative friends for a very civilised afternoon treat.

Clarke's Restaurant

122–124 Kensington Church Street, W8 4BH
☎ 020 7221 9225 www.sallyclarke.com
Open Monday–Friday 8am–11am,
12.30–2pm, 6.30pm–10pm, Saturday
8am–11am, 12–2pm, 6.30pm–10pm,
closed Bank Holidays **Tube** Notting Hill
Gate **Bus** 27, 28, 52, 70, 328, 452
The restaurant has wheelchair access

Sally Clarke has a formidable reputation
for her fresh, seasonal cooking. The
atmosphere in this beautiful, farm-to-
table restaurant is calm and the waiting
staff are attentive and courteous. It is
no wonder that Clarke's is one of the
first choices for diners who appreciate a
quiet meal alone or with friends.

William Morris Gallery Tea Room

Forest Road, Walthamstow E17 4PP
☎ 020 8496 4390
www.wmgallery.org.uk/visit/tea-room
Open Wednesday–Sunday 10am–4.30pm
Tube Blackhorse Road, Walthamstow
Central **Bus** 34, 97, 123, 215, 275, 357
The café is fully wheelchair accessible

The lovely William Morris Gallery Tea
Room is an ideal place to meet for lunch
or afternoon tea. With charming views
over Lloyd Park, this is a light-filled
space in which to enjoy a honey-glazed
root vegetable pie, fruit salad and
artisanal beer.

The Oasis Coffee Shop

The Salvation Army, Regent Hall, 275 Oxford Street, W1C 2DJ ☎ 020 7629 5424
www.regenthall.co.uk
Open Monday–Saturday 10am–4pm
Tube Oxford Circus **Bus** 2, 3, 6, 7, 8, 10, 12, 13, 15, 16, 25, 53, 94, 137, 139, 159
The café is fully wheelchair accessible

It is no wonder that this small, unassuming coffee shop is called the Oasis. Located near Oxford Circus, the two rooms are a peaceful haven for shoppers and local office workers who come here for baked potatoes, sandwiches and hot soups. The Oasis is one of the most reasonably priced cafés in London but is rarely busy. Most people who drop in for a cup of tea and cake speak rather quietly, as if they want to keep this a restful place for everyone who visits. If you also appreciate calming live music, free concerts are held at 1pm on Friday in the Regent Hall behind the café, where you may get to hear a flute duet or piano recital.

RADA Foyer Bar

Royal Academy of Dramatic Art, Malet Street entrance, Bloomsbury WC1E 6ED
☎ 020 7636 7076 (RADA main number)
www.rada.ac.uk/about/venue-hire/bar-cafe
Open Monday–Friday 10.30am–5pm; during productions Monday–Friday 10.30am–11pm, Saturday 12pm–11pm, closed Sundays
Tube Goodge Street, Euston Square **Bus** 7, 10, 14, 29, 73, 134, 188, 390
The café and theatre are wheelchair accessible

A small queue forms quite quickly just before midday when the hot dishes are brought out from the kitchen. Student actors, academics and other people working in the vicinity tend to keep this café a secret as it is such a nice place to meet up for lunch. To accompany a steaming bowl of hot chickpea ragoût, fill your plate with mixed root vegetables or fennel and green bean salads. This is also a good place to drop by for an early evening glass of wine or a pre-theatre dinner. Some evenings, you might even hear a recital or short performance in one corner of the café, but the atmosphere remains civilised and calm, whatever the event.

Petersham Nurseries Café

Petersham Road, Richmond, Surrey TW10 7AG ☎ 020 8940 5230
www.petershamnurseries.com
Open Shop and nursery Monday–Saturday 9am–5pm, Sunday 11am–5pm, lunch
reservations for café Tuesday–Sunday 12–3pm, teahouse Tuesday–Saturday 10am–
4.30pm, Sunday 11am–4.30pm, open most Bank Holidays except Easter Saturday,
Easter Sunday, Christmas Day and Boxing Day
Tube and **Train** Richmond **Bus** 65, 371
The nursery is on one level, except for steps into the teahouse. There is an accessible
toilet and allocated disabled parking outside

The beautiful Petersham Nurseries were created in the 1970s from a large, rambling
garden surrounding Petersham House. Under the direction of celebrated head chef
Skye Gingell, the sustainable restaurant opened in 2004 and was awarded a Michelin
star in 2012. The chefs source food from Petersham's own walled kitchen garden,
using edible flowers, herbs and heritage vegetables. Entrées might include smoked
haddock and chorizo salad or quinoa with grilled halloumi. The teahouse offers light,
Italian-inspired lunches as well as cakes and ethically sourced teas.

The Kew Greenhouse

1 Kew Station Parade, Richmond TW9 3PS ☎ 020 8940 0183
www.thekewgreenhousecafe.com
Open Daily 8am–6pm, summer evenings to 9pm, closed Christmas Day
Tube and **Train** Kew Gardens **Bus** 65, 190, 391, 419, R68
The café is wheelchair accessible

Built in 1895, the Kew Greenhouse used to be the village bakery and this attractive
tearoom overlooks the leafy village square near Kew Gardens. Everything is baked
on the premises and you'll find mainly traditional gâteaux on the menu as well as
baked vanilla cheesecake. This is one of the best places in London to have a clotted
cream tea with scones, jam and a pot of Darjeeling. The view from the conservatory is
delightful and on sunny days sitting at the pavement tables is a relaxing way to catch
some dappled sunshine though the trees. This is an excellent place to order lunch,
too, perhaps their celery and walnut roast or a slice of courgette and onion flan. If you
get an opportunity, have a look at the beautifully preserved old brick ovens with their
ornate cast iron doors and coke-fired furnaces in the old bakehouse at the rear.

COFFEE AND
WALNUT CAKE

£3.50

PLUM & ALMOND
TART

May Contain Traces of Nuts

£3.50

LEMON AND
POPPY DRIZZL
CAKE

May Contain Traces of Nu

£2

Dulwich Picture Gallery Café

Gallery Road, SE21 7AD ☎ 020 8299 8717
www.dulwichpicturegallery.org.uk/visit/dulwich-picture-gallery-café
Open Tuesday–Saturday 8am–5pm, Sunday 9.30am–5pm, closed Mondays,
Christmas Day, Boxing Day and New Year's Eve
Train West Dulwich, North Dulwich **Bus** P4
The café is fully wheelchair accessible

With its cool veined marble table-tops, black felted seating and pale stone floor, this is a very stylish café to enjoy a mid-morning coffee or afternoon tea. Professional chefs bake delicious cakes in-house, and their lemon and poppy seed drizzle cake and raspberry and white chocolate muffins are much admired. Located at the entrance to the idyllic grounds of Dulwich Picture Gallery, the first public art gallery in the country, this is a very civilised place to have a white bean and fennel salad lunch or just a glass of chilled elderflower pressé. The weekends can be very popular, so it is advisable to reserve a table in advance.

The Sea Shell of Lisson Grove

49–51 Lisson Grove, NW1 6UH ☎ 020 7224 9000
www.seashellrestaurant.co.uk
Open Monday–Saturday 12–10.30pm, closed Sundays
Tube Marylebone **Bus** 139, 189
A disabled access lift and toilets are available

With over eleven varieties of English-caught fish to choose from, it is no wonder that The Sea Shell of Lisson Grove has such a high reputation. People come here from all over London to try cod Panco, a Japanese-style flaky breadcrumb-fried fish, and their bite-sized 'popcorn' prawns. It's hard to choose between the freshly battered halibut, sea bass, haddock, rock salmon and Dover sole cooked in groundnut oil – all served with their inimitable chunky chips, a wedge of lemon and homemade tartare sauce. For a healthier option, you can ask for any fish to grilled with just a sprinkling of olive oil, and there are salads in the chill cabinet next to the marble counter. The adjoining restaurant plays background music, but this traditional fish and chip shop fortunately remains muzac-free.

Suzzle Café
47 Brick Lane, E1 6PU ☎ 07799 292 709
www.facebook.com/SuzzleUK
Open Monday–Friday 8am–6pm, Sunday 10am–6pm, closed Saturdays and
Bank Holidays
Tube Aldgate East **Bus** 15, 25, 115, 135, 205, 254
There is wheelchair access to the café

You would hardly notice, as the food is so varied and delicious here, but everything is gluten-free since the chef has to avoid wheat and other flours. Try their mango cake with passion fruit buttercream, or a slice of dairy free carrot and pistachio cake with a mug of hot chocolate. This very friendly café is a cool place to hang out at lunchtime. Their savoury pasties are appreciated not only by hungry locals but also by the artists Gilbert and George who often order a couple for their lunch. The artwork on the walls is usually exciting, unusual and hard to ignore.

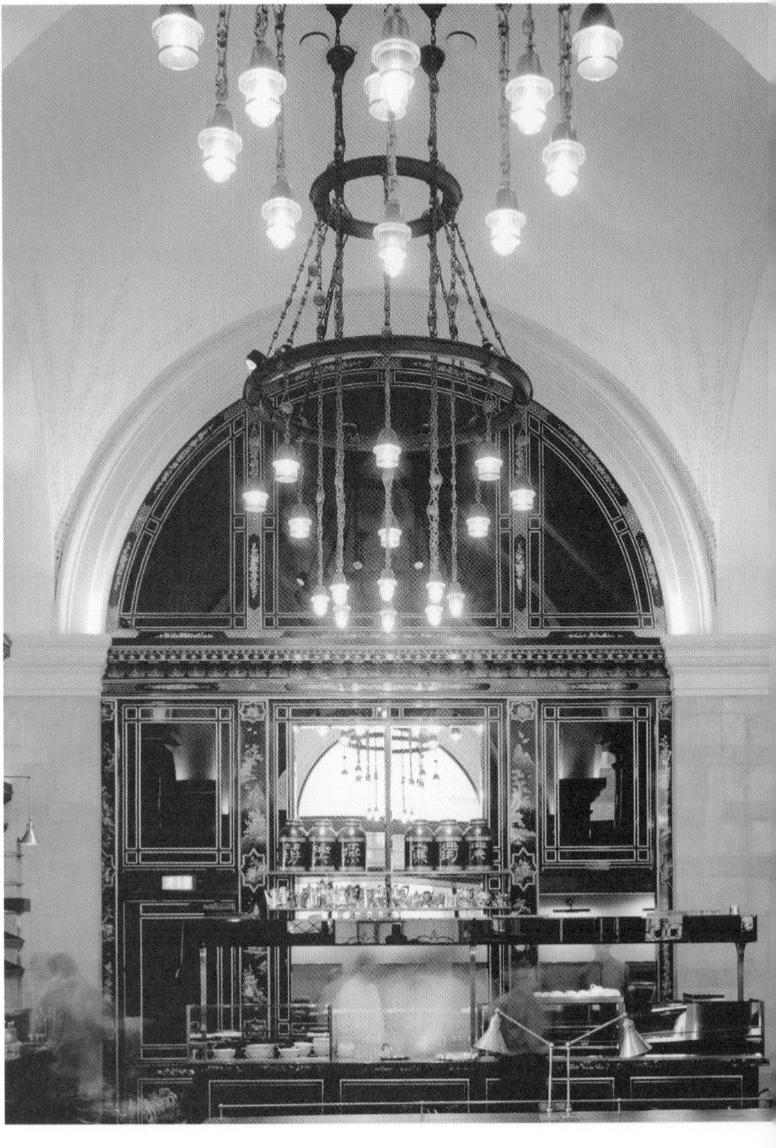

The Wolseley

160 Piccadilly, W1J 9EB ☎ 020 7499 6996
www.thewolseley.com
Open Monday–Friday 7–11.30am, 12–3pm, 5.30pm–12am, Saturday and Sunday
8–11.30am, 12–3.30pm, 5.30pm–12am (Sunday to 11pm)
Tube Green Park **Bus** 8, 9, 14, 19, 22, 38
The Wolseley is wheelchair accessible

It is hard to believe that this opulent, high-ceilinged café-restaurant on Piccadilly used to be a car showroom, but this is how it obtained its celebrated name. With its huge arched windows, grand ceiling lights and black-and-gold chinoiserie panels, this is the perfect English brasserie. The service is impeccable, and the dishes on the reasonably priced à la carte or all-day menus are inspired by the grand cafés of Europe. Their avocado and lamb's lettuce salad is an excellent starter, followed by seafood soup with mussels or chicken soup with dumplings. It is advisable to reserve a table in advance, especially for a Sunday morning breakfast of kedgeree or grilled kipper with mustard butter.

Small shops

Green Island Fresh Foods
47 Broadway Market, Hackney E8 4PH ☎ 07884 195 557
Open Daily 8am–9pm all year
Train Cambridge Heath, London Fields **Bus** 236
There is a 10cm step into the shop and a raised area at the rear

Green Island seems to have almost every ingredient you would ever want for a delicious supper or a summer picnic on nearby London Fields. They have a wide range of familiar vegetables, from red peppers to Cyprus potatoes as well as purple carrots, golden beetroot and exotic fruits such as kumquats and black figs. Many items are organic, such as the herbal teas and yoghurts, and you can always order things not in stock. One reason to shop here is that the owner selects the best-selling organic wines in Britain, so you don't have to ponder which one is best for an impromptu dinner party – whatever bottle you buy here will be appreciated by your guests.

Chegworth Farm Shop

221 Kensington Church Street, W8 7LX
☎ 0207 229 3016
www.chegworthvalley.com/our_shops
Open Monday–Saturday 8am–8pm,
Sunday 9am–6pm
Tube Notting Hill Gate
Bus 27, 28, 52, 70, 328, 390, 452
The shop is wheelchair accessible

It is no surprise that the shelves at the front of this organic grocers are full to the ceiling with bottles of Chegworth Farm juices. Raspberries, pears, apples and beetroots are all pressed in small batches on their family-run fruit farm in the Kent countryside.

Portobello Wholefoods

266 Portobello Road, W10 5TY
☎ 020 8968 9133
Open Monday–Saturday 9.30am–6pm,
Sunday 11am–5pm
Tube Ladbroke Grove
Bus 7, 23, 31, 70, 228
There is a ramp for wheelchair users

Portobello Wholefoods have been here for a few decades now, and their longevity is unsurprising. They have a very wide selection of grains, breakfast cereals and bottled drinks, ensuring that everyone's breakfast can be both healthy and delicious. Their eco toiletries range is also very good.

Bittersweet paprika

Mild paprika

Pimenton dulce

R. Garcia and Sons Delicatessen

248–250 Portobello Road, W11 1LL ☎ 020 7221 6119

www.rgarciaandsons.com

Open Sunday–Monday 10am–6pm, Tuesday–Saturday 9am–6pm

Tube Ladbroke Grove **Bus** 7, 10, 18, 31, 70, 228, 328, 452

There is a small step at the entrance but wheelchair users can usually manage this

Discovering R. Garcia and Sons is like finding edible treasure in the middle of London. Tins of anchovies, fresh olives, salty manchego cheese, almond turron, fig jam, squid ink and giant white beans are all waiting to be picked off the shelf. As well as a range of delicious staples, here you'll find produce not available anywhere else in London, such as Xorchata tiger nut drink and lemon cologne, both perfect on hot summer days when London feels as sultry as Madrid. In December, the shop is filled with extravagantly wrapped Spanish Christmas delicacies, making this the perfect place to buy delicious presents. The shop has been here for over sixty years and is so well stocked that Spaniards travel here from as far as Valencia and Seville to buy their padrón peppers and pickled garlic.

East London Sausage Company

57 Orford Road, Walthamstow E17 9NJ ☎ 020 8520 4060
Open Tuesday–Saturday 8.30am–7pm, Sunday 10am–2pm
Tube Walthamstow Central **Bus** 97, 257, 357, W11, W15, W16
The shop is wheelchair accessible

Every day of the week, a team of butchers are busy in the rear kitchens, stuffing 47 varieties of sausage. From Essex county pork to German bratworst, and strings of traditional Cumberland or Spanish chorizo, there are plenty to choose from. There is even a lemon, coriander and chicken sausage, but no vegetarian options in this meat emporium. Unusual versions include Highland venison with port and wild boar with forest fruits, and you can also pick up a box of free-range eggs and jars of locally made chutneys from the counter. One of the best ways to appreciate fast food which has been made slowly and carefully, sausages are an ideal supper dish.

Ganache Chocolatier

80 Brewer Street, Soho W1F 9TZ ☎ 020 7439 9119
Open Sunday–Thursday 10am–midnight, Friday and Saturday 10am–1am
Tube Piccadilly Circus **Bus** 3, 6, 12, 13, 14, 15, 19, 22, 23, 38, 88, 94, 139, 159, 453
There is wheelchair access to the shop and café, with two pavement tables outdoors

With over a hundred different chocolates to choose from, it is very difficult to know which ones to try first. From cocoa-dusted truffles to marzipan, almond, fondant and coffee centres, these Belgian chocolates are perfect miniature interval treats during an evening at the theatre. The small shop and café stays open late, so after a trip to the cinema you can drop in for some pistachio baklava and a macchiato. This small patisserie also has a huge range of Turkish delight, from pomegranate, sour cherry, mint and apple flavour to the more traditional rosewater and lemon. As well as maple syrup and walnut or raspberry waffle fudge, they also stock Turkish coffee, and sugar- and fat-free chocolates for diabetics and anyone who prefers a slightly less indulgent treat.

Panache Chocolate Shop

182–186 Kensington Church Street, W8 4DP ☎ 020 7235 8819
www.panache.co.uk **Open** Monday–Saturday 8.30am–8pm, Sunday 10am–5pm (until
6pm during summer and over the Christmas period)
Tube Notting Hill Gate **Bus** 27, 28, 52, 70, 94, 148, 328, 390, 452
There is one small step at the entrance to the shop and no access to the rear, but
staff can bring items for customers

Most of the chocolates in Panache are imported from France, and with over fifty
varieties behind the counter you are spoilt for choice. Staff will fill pretty boxes with
marron glacés, hazelnut praline, dark chocolate squares, marzipan delights and
chocolate-coated brazil nuts. This may be the only place in London you can buy
macaronio – mini versions of the quintessentially French macaroons. At the rear
of the shop you can find christening and baby shower gifts, including silver bowls,
crystal trinkets and elegant Czech glass vases. Whatever you buy here will be
beautifully wrapped by hand.

ASC
EST
1965
Quality Food Products
AMBALA®
The Finest Asian Confectionery

Ambala Foods

112–114 Drummond Street, NW1 2HN ☎ 020 7387 7886
www.ambalafoods.com **Open** Daily 9am–9pm
Tube Euston, Warren Street **Bus** 18, 24, 27, 29, 68, 88, 134, 153, 168, 476
The shop is wheelchair accessible and has automatic doors

This Drummond Street branch is probably the quietest of Ambala's six London shops selling Pakistani and Indian sweets and savouries. It is hard to walk out of the door without buying a few slices of crisp walnut baklawa dripping with syrup. If you are ever at a loss about what gifts to take to a dinner party, some succulent rasgulla, jalebis and rich, milky barfis and carrot halwas would delight any host. For weddings or Eid celebrations, take a box of gold-wrapped urad ladoo with their sweet, nutty texture. And for a very cheap, filling lunch, a bag of hot cauliflower and potato pakoras go very well with a jar of Ambala's own chilli and mango mixed pickle.

Carmelli Bakery
126–128 Golders Green Road, NW11 8HB ☎ 020 8455 2789
www.carmelli.co.uk
Open Sunday–Friday 6am–1am, closed Saturday and Jewish holidays
Tube Golders Green **Bus** 83, 102, 210, 268, 460
The shop is wheelchair accessible

Danish pastries, smoked salmon bagels and chocolate croissants are piled high in this kosher bakery in Golders Green. This is a convivial place to pick up a lunchtime snack or a cholla bread on your way home from work. They stay open late most nights of the week, so you don't have to worry about hunger pangs after a trip to the cinema. The shop has won prizes for its delicious rugelach and cheesecakes, and for a quick lunch you can take away a couscous dish or a freshly baked vegetable quiche. In the chill cabinet you can also find dairy-free cakes for a special occasion.

The Grocer on Elgin

6 Elgin Crescent, W11 2HX ☎ 020 7221 3844
www.thegroceron.com
Open Monday–Friday 7am–8pm, Saturday 7am–7pm, Sunday 7am–6pm
Tube Ladbroke Grove **Bus** 7, 23, 31, 228, 295, 452
There is a small step at the door but help is available

The Grocer on Elgin is one of a small chain of three independent London grocers which offer excellent produce to anyone who loves to eat delicious food. From their artisanal breads in the window to the cheese quiches and berry tarts on slate platters, this is a dream location for gourmets. This branch also has a small café at the rear, where professional chefs create dishes to tempt even the most fussy eaters. Their beetroot and quince soup is an unusual interpretation of a classic dish and you can also have pizza or a plate of ratatouille. After a morning coffee, why not do your weekly shop here? Fill up on dried pasta, empanadas, organic eggs, raspberries, olive oil, fresh tomatoes and halloumi cheese parcels.

Cheeses

13 Fortis Green Road, Muswell Hill N10 3HP ☎ 020 8444 9141
www.cheesesonline.co.uk
Open Monday–Saturday 10am–5pm
Tube East Finchley **Bus** 43, 102, 134, 144, 184, 234, W7
The shop is accessible but is very narrow. There's an accessible pavement stall
outside on Saturdays from 10am

Even if the sight of white camembert and blue-veined Stilton in the window doesn't
lure you inside this specialist cheese shop, the pungent smell of ripening Colston
Bassett coming from the interior probably will. This is a good place to ask about the
provenance of each cheese and to find out about the best one for your particular
palate. Or you can just drop by and pick up a soft ewe's milk to spread on an oat
cracker with a glass of red wine later on. Here you can find mustards by Wiltshire
Tracklements, cheese slates and bars of dark chocolate. On Saturday, pick up a
crusty olive flute baguette and sample what's on offer that day from the street stall.
Look out for the traditional rounds of cheese underneath the blue umbrella.

Earth Natural Foods

100 Kentish Town Road, NW5 2AE ☎ 020 7482 2211
www.earthnaturalfoods.co.uk
Open Monday–Saturday 8.30am–7pm, Sunday 11am–5pm
Tube Kentish Town **Train** Kentish Town West **Bus** 134, 214, C2
The shop is wheelchair accessible

Earth Natural Foods are a well-established organic grocers offering a wide selection of dry goods, toiletries, household cleaning products and fresh fruit and vegetables. Their sourdough whole wheat and olive ciabatta loaves are very popular, as are their blueberry tarts and mini quiches. At the back of the shop, you can also order hot, tasty lunches from the counter. There's always a good choice, from tomato soup to lentil and spinach ragu and their rather decadent absinthe and chocolate cake. You could do your entire weekly shop here and not have to endure supermarket queues ever again.

Algerian Coffee Stores

2 Old Compton Street, W1D 4PB ☎ 020 7437 2480
www.algcoffee.co.uk
Open Monday–Wednesday 9am–7pm, Thursday and Friday 9am–9pm, Saturday
9am–8pm, closed Bank Holidays except for Good Friday
Tube Leicester Square, Piccadilly Circus **Bus** 6, 7, 14, 24, 29, 38, 73, 159, 390
There is a small step at the entrance but help is available to get into the shop

The Algerian Coffee Stores have been here since 1887 when Mr Hassan, the first
owner, came from Algiers to set up business as a coffee trader. The company has
remained in the family for decades, and with over 120 different coffees and 120 kinds
of teas, it would be hard to leave without finding something to please your palate. As
well as Argentinan Maté, pink Earl Grey and smoked Assam, the shop has one of the
largest selections of flowering tea balls in London. Opening up like mini gardens in a
teapot filled with hot water, these unusual leaf concoctions make discerning presents
for tea lovers. If you prefer to wake up to a morning cup of coffee, you can ask for
Ethiopian longberry or South American Honduras beans to be freshly ground and
wrapped up in a brown paper bag.

La Plaza Deli

288 Portobello Road, W10 5TE ☎ 020 8968 0900
Open Daily 9am–7pm including Easter, closed Christmas Day, Boxing Day and
New Year's Day
Tube Ladbroke Grove, Westbourne Park **Bus** 28, 52, 70, 295, 452
The shop is not wheelchair accessible due to the steps at the front door

One of two well-stocked Spanish delicatessens on Portobello Road, La Plaza looks
like a corner shop filled with the most tempting of Galician delicacies. Cured hams
and huge paella pans hang from ceiling hooks, while the shelves are tightly packed
with Santiago almond tarts, salted almonds, saffron, paella rice, Rioja, Manzanilla
sherry, pimientos, tinned octopus and olive oils. One of the fresh items that can't
be found in many British grocers are small green peppers, a spicy addition to any
Mediterranean meal.

Fernandez & Wells

43 Lexington Street, W1F 9AL ☎ 020 7734 1546
www.fernandezandwells.com **Open** Monday–Friday 7.30am–11pm, Saturday 9am–
11pm, Sunday 9am–6pm **Tube** Piccadilly Circus, Leicester Square **Bus** 14, 19, 38
There is a small step at the door and the deli is not very spacious but staff are willing
to help

Behind the stripped oak counter hang large Iberia hams just waiting to be thinly
sliced for a sophisticated Spanish sandwich. As well as cured meats, the cheeses in
this stylish delicatessen are quite exceptional. Their organic Parmegiano Reggiano is
made by Umberto Avanzini and his family in the foothills of the Parma Apennines with
milk from Swiss cows. Every product is very carefully sourced, from the soft, wet balls
of water buffalo mozzarella from just south of Naples, to two-day fermented potato
honey focaccia made by the Seven Seeded Artisan Bakery. This is also an excellent
place to buy wine by the glass or bottle, smoked anchovies, Oloroso sherry, Eccles
cakes and hand-made preserves.

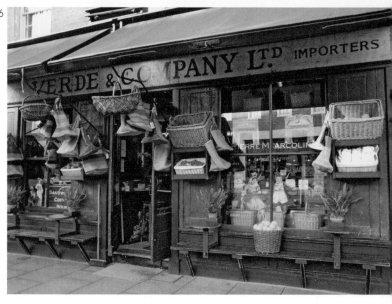

Verde & Company

40 Brushfield Street, E1 6AG ☎ 020 7247 1924
www.verdeandco.co.uk **Open** Daily 9am–6pm
Tube Liverpool Street **Bus** 8, 26, 35, 42, 47, 48, 67, 78, 135, 149, 242, 344, 388
There is a 12cm step at the entrance but staff can bring food to the tables outside

This is a lovely old-fashioned shop with a sophisticated, cool edge. Whether you are
buying succulent gifts for friends or just treating yourself to some rose-petal preserve
and Chardonnay vinegar, even looking at the tempting packaged food on the shelves
is a real pleasure. In one corner, semi-translucent jars of marmalade glow orange
when the sun shines, and in winter you can warm yourself by the fire in the hearth.
A cross between a cosy living room filled with heirloom furniture (the owner inherited
the roll-top desk), and a bijoux café, this is the perfect place to drop by for Italian
biscuits, glacé fruits, almond cakes and Pierre Marcolini chocolates. You can also
have lunch here, or pick up a goats cheese and red pepper flan to take away.

I Camisa & Son

61 Old Compton Street, W1D 6HS ☎ 020 7437 7610
Open Monday–Saturday 8.30am–6pm
Tube Leicester Square, Tottenham Court Road **Bus** 14, 19, 38
The shop is wheelchair accessible but quite small

I Camisa is a Soho institution – people travel from miles around to pick up their groceries in this wonderful Italian deli. The shelves are densely packed with black squid ink spaghetti, Baci chocolates, dried herbs, Sapori panforte, Toscano farro, bottles of Chianti, catuccini alla mandorla and even franchi seeds to grow your own basil or green beans. Staff will gladly weigh out the freshly made spinach taglierini, grilled courgettes and Tuscan pecorino cheese, and slice off a piece of focaccia to go with your fresh rocket and tomato salad. If it's too cold for a picnic, you can also pick up some fresh tomato and porcini mushroom sauce, which will go perfectly with potato gnocchi and buffalo mozzarella after a starter of marinated anchovies. One nice touch is the traditional sawdust on the floor – this a much more intimate way to shop than in big supermarket chains.

OSTERLEY
PARK
FARM
E
SUNFLOWER
SEED HEADS
£1 EACH
MARROW
£1-00 EACH

Osterley Park Farm Shop

Jersey Road, Isleworth TW7 4RB ☎ 020 8560 6580
Open Daily 11am–5pm
Train Isleworth **Bus** H28, H91
The outdoor greengrocers is weelchair accessible

After a visit to the magnificent National Trust Neoclassical mansion inside Osterley Park, you might want to do some grocery shopping at this outdoor farm shop, located on the small road leading to the grand house. The fruit and vegetables here are not organic but they are very cheap and most are locally produced, including the eggs. As well as giant marrows, desirée potatoes and bags of tomatoes, you can also pick up large dried sunflower heads, packed full of seeds for garden birds to nibble on throughout the winter months.

Gate Delicatessen (Deli & Delights)

343 Archway Road, N6 5AA ☎ 0208 340 8632
www.delianddelights.co.uk
Open Monday–Friday 9am–7pm, Saturday 9am–6pm closed Christmas Day, New Year's Day, Easter Sunday and Monday
Tube Highgate **Bus** 43, 134, 203, 603
There is an 8cm-step at the entrance but ramps are available for customers, the rear room is not accessible but staff can bring items to your basket

This friendly deli close to Highgate Station has one of the largest selection of gourmet foods in London. The front part of the shop stocks specialist savoury crackers, rainbow pasta, and artisanal stoneground bread whilst the rear is filled with baskets piled high with fresh fruit and vegetables below shelves heaving with olive oils and wine vinegars. Deli & Delights has been here for over 25 years and specialises in German chocolates and cakes and Austrian sweets such as marzipan pigs. This is not just a great place to do a weekly shop but also the ideal location for delicious presents for discerning friends.

The People's Supermarket

72–76 Lamb's Conduit Street, WC1N 3LP ☎ 020 7430 1827
www.thepeoplessupermarket.org
Open Monday–Saturday 8am–10pm, Sunday 8am–9pm
Tube Russell Square **Bus** 17, 25, 46, 242, 341
The shop is wheelchair accessible

This is a exciting concept – a well-stocked, central London supermarket run and
supported by local people. Loyal members work here a few hours a week and the
People's Supermarket has the feel of a corner shop but with the range and variety
of a medium-sized supermarket. Their range of fruit and vegetables is excellent
– with two sorts of peach in summer, and cucumbers that taste better than those
in conventional supermarkets. Look out for giant garlic bulb stems and boxes of
delicious English apples in autumn. Using seasonal produce throughout the year,
a local chef produces scrumptious hot lunches to take away at the back of the
shop. This is not just a mecca for staff working at the nearby Great Ormond Street
Children's Hospital, but for people from all over the area.

Spitalfields Organics

103 Commercial Street, E1 6LZ ☎ 020 7377 8909
Open Daily 10am–7.30pm
Tube Liverpool Street **Train** Shoreditch High Street **Bus** 67
The shop is wheelchair accessible

Although there aren't any fresh vegetables or fruit in this unpretentious grocers, it's a good place to stock up on pesticide-free store cupboard items. Spitalfields Organics has the atmosphere of a corner shop but with all the produce found in larger health food stores. If you have just run out of free-range eggs, peppermint tea, jars of roasted aubergines, miso, sunflower seed rye bread, hummus and breakfast oats, you can find them on the shelves here. On hot summer days, this is also a good place to pick up an iced coffee and an organic ice cream to eat in Spitalfields Church gardens nearby. You can also find washing-up liquid and beauty products in abundance.

Sally Clarke Shop

1 Campden Street, W8 7EP ☎ 020 7229 2190
www.sallyclarke.com/shop
Open Monday–Friday 8am–8pm, Saturday 8am–5pm, Sunday 10am–4pm
Tube Notting Hill Gate **Bus** 27, 28, 31, 52, 70, 94, 148, 328, 452
There is a small step at the entrance to the shop

Sally Clarke's reputation as one of Britain's top bakers is well deserved and this small
shop offers food lovers a chance to buy a jar of her dark Seville orange marmalade
to spread on her slowly fermented sourdough loaves. Only the highest quality
ingredients are used to make the pickles, jams and jellies that sit on the shelves
in this pretty store, which stocks much more than teatime treats and breakfast
provisions. For lunch, pick up a tomato and mozzarella pizza made in their own pastry
kitchen and a lemon tart and a packet of Assam tea for later on that afternoon.

FAM Fruit and Vegetable Market

150 Fortess Road, Kentish Town NW5 2HP ☎ 020 7267 2046
Open Daily 7am–10pm
Tube Tufnell Park **Bus** 134, 214, 390, C2, C11
The shop is weelchair accessible

Whether you are looking for ripe tomatoes and red onions for a ragù or a cos lettuce and radishes for a summer salad, FAM have every vegetable you would ever need. The bunches of verdant spinach-like saag, dill, mint and parsley look so fresh, it feels as if you have picked them yourself. As well as Cox apples, physalis, prickly pears, giant quince, star fruit and lychees, this is also a great place to buy balsamic vinegar, olive oil, rosewater and other bottled produce. The food is very reasonably priced, even fruits that have travelled far, such as pomegranates and persimmons.

Pubs & bars

Ashburnham Arms

25 Ashburnham Grove, Greenwich, SE10 8UH ☎ 020 8355 5141
www.ashburnham-arms.co.uk
Open Monday–Friday 4pm–12am, Saturday 12pm–12am, Sunday 12–11pm
DLR Greenwich **Bus** 53, 177, 180, 199, 386
There is a ramp for wheelchair users – ring in advance for access. The ground floor toilets are small, however.

This elegant public house is one of the most attractive pubs in London. Not far from Deptford Creek, the Asburnham Arms is a hidden secret much appreciated by locals and beer aficionados. Located on a play street, the road outside is quieter than many in Greenwich. In warmer weather, sit in the conservatory or in the beer garden at the rear. It might get busy in summer, so come early for their baked pizzas, fish and chips, and chicken pie and mash. This is a great local pub to sit and enjoy a selection of Shepherd Neame's fine ales and lagers, as well as some excellent home cooked bar meals. If you prefer a quiet evening out, avoid times when a rugby match is on, as this will be screened on their large screen television.

The Coach & Horses

29 Greek Street, Soho W1D 5DH ☎ 020 7437 5920
www.thecoachandhorsessoho.co.uk
Open Monday–Thursday 11am–11pm, Friday and Saturday 10am–12am, Sunday 12–
10.30pm **Tube** Leicester Square **Bus** 19, 14, 24, 29, 38, 176
The pub is wheelchair accessible

Renowned for being London's first vegetarian pub, this Soho landmark is an excellent
place to enjoy gourmet food in an informal atmosphere. The pub also has a notorious
history – Peter O'Toole, Francis Bacon, the columnist Jeffrey Bernard, *Private Eye*
magazine journalists and louche Soho personalities all came here to argue over the
rambunctious politics of the day. Nowadays, it tends to be more sedate, especially
on a Sunday lunchtime. Their nut roast is a tasty alternative to the meat and two veg
offerings elsewhere, and their weekday menu of beetroot ravioli and apple and plum
crumble are also much appreciated. Piano singalongs take place on Wednesday and
Saturday – the only time you will hear music in this well-loved pub.

The French House

49 Dean Street, Soho W1D 5BG ☎ 020 7494 2477
www.frenchhousesoho.com
Open Monday–Saturday 12–11pm, Sunday 12–10.30pm, Christmas Day to 2pm,
New Year's Eve to 9pm, food served Monday–Friday 12–3.30pm
Tube Leicester Square, Piccadilly Circus, Tottenham Court Road
Bus 14, 19, 24, 29, 38, 176
The pub is wheelchair accessible but not very large

The French House opened in 1914, and was like a second home to anyone fleeing
France during the Second World War. The pub is also famous for being a meeting
place for actors and the walls are covered with photos of former guests. The cosy
atmosphere is partly due to the fact that the pub is quite small, but also because
regulars come here often to meet their compatriots and enjoy a pint of Old Speckled
Hen. In keeping with the Gallic tradition of drinking smaller glasses of beer, the pub
serves only half-pints. During the week, the French House serves an excellent three-
course lunch, and on special occasions a pianist plays in this historic bar.

The Star Tavern

6 Belgrave Mews, SW1X 8HT
☎ 020 7235 3019
www.star-tavern-belgravia.co.uk
Open Monday–Friday 11am–11pm,
Saturday 12–11pm, Sunday 12–10.30pm,
closed New Year's Day
Tube Knightsbridge, Hyde Park Corner
Bus 14, 22, 38, 73, 137, 360, 452, C1
There is a small step at the entrance

With fresh flowers on the tables,
excellent home-cooked food and
seasonal ales, this popular, award-
winning Fuller's pub is much loved
by locals. The only remaining pub in
Mayfair with a real coal fire, it's a great
place to retire to on a winter's evening.

The Windmill

6–8 Mill Street, Mayfair, W1S 2AZ
☎ 020 7491 8050
www.windmillmayfair.co.uk
Open Monday–Saturday 11.45am–11pm,
Sunday 12–6pm
Tube Oxford Circus **Bus** 6, 10, 23, 55, 73,
88, 98, 139, 159, 453, C2
The pub is on the ground floor but has
no accessible toilets

The Windmill is famous for its award-
winning pies, which include smoked
haddock and crayfish as well as the
traditional steak and kidney. With its
polished brass fittings and gold and
white ceiling, this is a comfortable
place to have a lunchtime pint.

The Fitzroy Tavern

16a Charlotte Street, Fitzrovia W1T 2LY ☎ 020 7580 3714
Open Monday–Saturday 11am–11pm, Sunday 12–10.30pm
Tube Goodge Street, Warren Street **Bus** 10, 14, 24, 29, 73, 134, 390
The ground floor of the pub is wheelchair accessible but the toilets are down a flight
of stairs

Renowned for having some of the cheapest pints in central London, this traditional
nineteenth-century public house is a great place to meet up with friends. The large
bar on the ground floor is surrounded by typical wooden pub tables and chairs, while
the small basement room is much more intimate. Eric Blair, better known as George
Orwell, used to come to the Fitzroy Tavern for a drink while he was writing his articles
and novels, and the pub still attracts a literary clientele. On Wednesday it hosts the
very lively Pear Shaped Comedy Club, but every other night of the week this is a
sedate place to enjoy a real ale or their summer fruit cup.

The Knights Templar

95 Chancery Lane, WC2A 1DT ☎ 020 7831 2660
www.jdwetherspoon.co.uk/home/pubs/the-knights-templar-chancery-lane
Open Monday–Wednesday 8am–11pm, Thursday–Friday 8am–11.30pm, Saturday 11am–6pm, closed on Sunday except for private events
Tube Chancery Lane **Bus** 1, 11, 15, 63, 76, 341, 521
The pub is fully wheelchair accessible

Built as the Grand Union bank in the 1840s, the Knights Templar was transformed into a public house a hundred and fifty years later. This listed building feels quite spectacular with its beautiful red-painted ceiling, gold capitals at the top of the columns and tulip-shaped ceiling lights. The menu covers the entire day, from a large cooked breakfast to a club sandwich for lunch and a curry after work. With six to eight varieties on tap and a beer festival in the autumn, this is a great pub to try out an American Bitter, an Abbott IPA or one of their guest ales. Although there is a television screen on during the day, it is turned to silent, with only subtitles offering the latest news.

The Royal Oak

44 Tabard Street, Borough SE1 4JU ☎ 020 7357 7173
www.harveys.org.uk/pubs/the-royal-oak-london
Open Monday–Friday 11am–11pm, Saturday 12–11pm, Sunday 12–9pm,
open Christmas Day, limited opening New Year's Day
Tube Borough **Bus** 21, 40, 133
There is a ramp for wheelchair users

With its simple dark wooden tables and chairs and handsome central bar, the Royal
Oak is an old-fashioned corner pub in a quiet back street near Borough tube. Owned
by Harvey's of Lewes, the beers here tend to have a southern English flavour. The ales
are the main attraction – you can sample a South Downs Harvest Ale, a Sussex Best
Bitter or a pale ale, all on tap and brewed by an independent. If you prefer a sweeter
taste, try a glass of Thatcher's Heritage cider to go with your ploughman's lunch. Just
keep an eye on your Stilton cheese and crusty bloomer bread, as quiet dogs are also
welcome here and they might also be partial to a freshly made sandwich.

White Wine OF THE MONTH
Chateaumeillant blanc, loire
FRANCE (2011)
A blend of 80% Sauvignon +
20% Chardonnay. This is like
Sancere crossed w/Chablis. £22⁰⁰

Red Wine OF THE MONTH
Ibiza tinto, Granada SPAIN
A blend of temp, Syrah (2010)
Cab Sauv & Merlot - this intense
cherry red is fermented in
american oak barrels.
Scents of cassis, liquorice + cocoa. £21⁰⁰

The Junction Tavern

101 Fortess Road, NW5 1AG ☎ 020 7485 9400
www.junctiontavern.co.uk
Open Monday–Thursday 5–11pm, Friday and Saturday 12pm–12am, Sunday 12–11pm,
New Year's Day, closed Christmas Eve and Christmas Day
Tube Tufnell Park **Bus** 134, 214, 390, C2, C11
The gastro pub is wheelchair accessible but the toilet door is very narrow

This impressive Victorian pub has been transformed into one of North London's most desirable restaurants. With its simple school chairs, bare tables, wood-panelled walls, plaster cornices, white candles and red plush bar stools the look is a mixture of informal bistro and traditional English public house. Beers on tap include Betty Stogs Queen of Cornish ale, San Miguel and Adnams Lighthouse, while the wine list includes cabernet sauvignon and chenin blanc. The food on the menu is typically English, so on Sunday you can expect roast beef and Yorkshire pudding, with lighter meals during the week. The rear conservatory and garden are also pleasant places to sit, with a few simple wooden benches and Russian vines climbing up the walls.

The Churchill Arms

119 Kensington Church Street, W8 7LN ☎ 020 7727 4242
www.churchillarmskensington.co.uk
Open Monday–Wednesday 11am–11pm, Thursday–Saturday 11am–midnight,
Sunday 12–10.30pm
Tube Notting Hill Gate **Bus** 27, 28, 52, 328, 452
The pub is not wheelchair accessible as there are two steps at the entrance

Built in 1750, The Churchill Arms has seen many eminent Londoners pass through
its doors, including the indomitable Winston Churchill. One of London's most famous
pubs, it's hard to miss, with its spectacular array of hanging baskets filled with
geraniums and yellow blossom. Winner of 'London in Bloom' two years in a row, the
Churchill Arms is also famed for its real ales and is a very convivial place to have a
Fuller's or a guest beer. In the conservatory at the back you can also order a delicious
Kaeng Par Thai curry or a dish of Pad Siew noodles.

The Bree Louise

69 Cobourg Street, NW1 2HH ☎ 0207 681 4930
www.thebreelouise.com
Open Monday–Saturday 11.30am–11pm, Sunday 12–10.30pm, food served 12–8.45pm
daily **Tube** Euston, Euston Square, Warren Street
Bus 10, 18, 24, 27, 29, 30, 73, 88, 134, 168, 205, 253, 390
The pub is wheelchair accessible

This pub has won many awards, both for its real ales and its seasonal turkey and
cranberry pies. If you enjoy tasting different hand-crafted beers, this is the ideal place
to bring your friends. The Bree Louise has eleven gravity ales and six pump beers,
as well as a number of real ciders and perry. Beers on tap might change throughout
the day as each barrel empties, giving drinkers an opportunity to try something
new if their favourite has just run out. The kind of people who come here are those
who appreciate excellent beers and good conversation in simple, unpretentious
surroundings. Spend a convivial evening at one of the wooden tables, with a pint
or two of the pub's own organic pilsner and a wild boar burger.

The Dispensary

19 Leman Street, Whitechapel E1 8EN ☎ 020 7977 0486
www.thedispensarylondon.co.uk
Open Monday–Friday 11.30am–11pm, closed Bank Holidays
Tube Green Park **Bus** 8, 9, 14, 19, 22, 38
The pub is not wheelchair accessible

Although loud music is played in the main bar, at the right of the entrance there is a much quieter small room where you can meet friends away from the clamour. The pub has recently been renovated but retains many of its nineteenth-century features, such as tiled floors and beaded fire surrounds. Beers rotate frequently and might include Hophead, Dark Star and a few others from independent breweries. The food here is excellent, from tomato and pesto soup to homemade ice cream. And if you want a very quiet place to eat, you can book the private dining room upstairs. Don't miss their fresh mint tea, one of the few places you can order this in London.

Nicolas Wine Bar

480 One Canada Square, E14 5AX ☎ bar 020 7512 9283, shop 020 7512 9092
www.nicolas.co.uk
Open Wine bar Monday–Friday 12–10pm, shop Monday–Friday 10am–8pm, Saturday
11am–7pm, closed Christmas Day, Boxing Day and New Year's Day
DLR Canary Wharf **Bus** 135, D3, D8
The wine bar and shop are both wheelchair accessible

With its burgundy-coloured seating, wooden floor, vintage Nicolas posters and
uncluttered interior, this is a stylish place to enjoy a glass of wine with friends after
work. With around twenty to order by the glass or three hundred by the bottle, the
knowledgeable staff can advise on the best wines to suit your palate. The focus is on
French vintages, from a Château de l'Engarran Grès de Montpellier 2010 to a Ruinart
Blanc de Blancs brut champagne made with chardonnay and pinot noir grapes. Food
is served at lunchtime, with hearty French dishes the main attraction on the menu.
Enjoy a cheese platter to share, or a beef stew followed by a tarte aux pommes.

The Hand in Hand

6 Crooked Billet, Wimbledon Common SW19 4RQ ☎ 020 8946 5720
www.thehandinhandwimbledon.co.uk
Open Monday–Thursday 11am–11pm, Friday–Saturday 11am–midnight,
Sunday 12–11pm
Tube and **Train** Wimbledon **Bus** 57, 93, 200
The pub is wheelchair accessible

In 1831 the Hand in Hand was described as a bakehouse, but it has been a Young's pub
for many years now. Situated on the edge of Wimbledon Common and overlooking
the village green, this is a very sociable, relaxing place to come and enjoy a pint on
a summer's evening. As well as Bombadier, Young's Gold, Sam Brooks, Hackney
Old Gold and ales from the London Fields brewery, a wide range of bottled beers
and wines is also served. The home-cooked food is very good here. Try their
field mushroom, red pepper and aubergine burger or the traditional chicken and
mushroom pie and ploughman's lunch. This pub is very dog-friendly and even sells
rawhide bones for its canine guests.

The George Inn

77 Borough High Street, Southwark SE1 1NH ☎ 020 7407 2056
www.nationaltrust.org.uk/george-inn
Open Monday–Saturday 11am–11pm, Sunday 12–10.30pm, food served 11am–10pm
Tube London Bridge, Borough **Bus** 17, 21, 40, 133
There is a small step at the entrance and the toilets are not easily accessible

This half-timbered Grade I-listed coaching inn dates from the seventeenth century and is the only remaining galleried inn in London. Charles Dickens came here when it was a coffee house in the nineteenth century and, with its illustrious history, the building is now owned by the National Trust. Nowadays, you can try one of their nine cask ales, either the George Inn's own brew, a Greene King IPA, or one of their seasonal beers. The inn has a wide range of bottled ales, including Golden Sheep, Noble and Old Speckled Hen. Good food is cooked daily in the kitchen, with pub favourites such as tasty fish pie and sirloin steak on the menu.

Goodman's Field
87–91 Mansell Street, E1 8AN
☎ 020 7680 2850
www.jdwetherspoon.co.uk/home/pubs/
goodmans-field **Open** Monday–Friday
7.30am–11pm, Saturday and Sunday
8am–11pm **Tube** Aldgate, Aldgate East
DLR Tower Gateway **Bus** 15, 25, 40, 67,
100, 115, 205, 254
Wheelchair accessible, step to toilets

This modern pub feels welcoming and
spacious and is excellent for anyone
who appreciates quiet surroundings.
Coffee, cream cheese bagels and
porridge with honey and apricots
make a hearty Sunday breakfast.

Penderel's Oak
283–288 High Holborn, WC1V 7HP
☎ 020 7242 5669 www.jdwetherspoon.
co.uk/home/pubs/penderels-oak
Open Monday–Wednesday 8am–11.30pm,
Thursday 8am–12pm, Friday–Saturday
8am–1am, Sunday 10am–10.30pm
Tube Holborn, Chancery Lane
Bus 8, 11, 19, 25, 38, 55, 98, 242
The pub is wheelchair accessible

Despite being in the centre of busy
Holborn, this comfortable modern inn
has a homely atmosphere. One of the
Weatherspoon chain of pubs, it plays
no background music – you'll just hear
the quiet hum of people talking.

he White Horse

3 Parsons Green, Fulham SW6 4UL ☎ 020 7736 2115 www.whitehorsesw6.com
pen Sunday–Wednesday 9.30am–11.30pm, Thursday–Saturday 9.30am–midnight
ube Parson's Green **Bus** 11, 14, 22, 295, 414, 424
he pub has excellent wheelchair access on the ground floor

enowned for its sunny beer garden and convivial atmosphere, this large Victorian
ub is a great place to meet up with friends in music-free surroundings. It can get
ery busy during Fulham and Chelsea home matches but at other times the pub is a
iendly location to chat, play card games and enjoy a pint. Their daily menu suggests
e perfect drink to accompany each dish, making it easy to try out new combinations
 beers, savoury dishes and puddings. Try their pan-fried scallops, cauliflower, apple
nd horseradish with an Anchor Liberty ale, or a roasted squash and endive salad
ith pine nuts and roast tomato chilli jam accompanied by a Blanche de Bruxelles
hite beer. This is also a wonderful place to learn about the drinks you are ordering,
 the staff run regular wine tastings as well as Beer Academy brewing courses.

Spinach & ...
Quiche
£3.00 or 2 for £5

Butternut Squash &
Cheddar Cheese Tart
£3 or 2 for £5.00

Food markets

Bloomsbury Farmers' Market

Torrington Square/Byng Place, behind University of London Students Union,
WC1E 7HY ☎ London Farmers' Markets 020 7833 0338
www.lfm.org.uk/markets/bloomsbury
Open Thursday 9am–2pm, closed Bank Holidays
Tube Goodge Street, Euston Square **Bus** 7, 10, 14, 24, 29, 73, 134, 188, 390
The market is wheelchair accessible

Once a week, this thriving market transforms the square behind ULU into a bustling
place to pick up a delicious hot meal or some incredibly fresh fruit and vegetables.
The Bath Soft Cheese Company bring their famous West Country cheeses to the
capital, some of which are made from recipes going back hundreds of years. Their
Somerset Brie is as tasty as the white rounds found in French fromageries – with
a loaf of rye bread, you are halfway to an alfresco lunch. Sit on the low walls
surrounding the square to enjoy your pheasant ravioli or, if it seems a bit crowded,
take an Artisan Food's broccoli, walnut and Stilton tart to another leafy square nearby.

Walthamstow Farmers' Market / Plot 44

Town Hall Square by Selbourne Walk Shopping Centre, off the High Street,
Walthamstow E17 7JN
☎ London Farmers' Markets 020 7833 0338, Plot 44 020 8531 0264
www.lfm.org.uk/markets/walthamstow, www.plotfortyfour.co.uk
Open Sunday 10am–2pm, closed Christmas Day, Boxing Day and New Year's Day
Tube Walthamstow Central **Bus** 20, 48, 69, 97, 212, 230, 257, 357, W15, W19
The market is wheelchair accessible

Walthamstow Farmers' market has been in Town Hall Square for seven years now,
and has a devoted following of locals who come for the biodynamic eggs and Millets
farm apples. Plot 44 is one of the stalwarts who turns up, rain or shine, whenever he
has a pitch. Sam Cork has a local allotment – number 44 to be exact – and he cooks
small, tasty batches of jams, chutneys, ketchups, relishes and pickles. As well as
Indian spicy chutney and cauliflower-crunchy piccalilli, he has been experimenting
with different flavours of jam: popular combinations include tempting jars of summer
elderflower, rhubarb and gooseberry and an autumnal blackberry and apple.

Islington Farmers' Market / Keik

Chapel Market, between Baron Street and Penton Street, N1 9PZ
☎ London Farmers' Markets 020 7833 0338, Keik 07758 461598
www.lfm.org.uk/markets/islington, www.keikltd.co.uk
Open Sunday 10am–2pm, closed Christmas Day, Boxing Day and New Year's Day
Tube Angel **Bus** 30, 73, 153, 214, 274, 394, 476, 812
The market is wheelchair accessible

The oldest of all the London farmers' markets, this Sunday morning collection of
stalls is also one of the busiest. Get there early for beautiful seasonal flowers, ripe
red, yellow and dark green tomatoes and organic courgettes so fresh their skins feel
squeaky when you pick them up. Keik have been cooking vegetable strudels, moist
coconut cakes and other delicious things to eat for over a year now, and this eye-
catching stall is one of the main attractions. The chef lays out her baked goods
on simple grey slates and they are usually all gone before lunchtime, so if you want
a delicious brunch but are feeling too lazy to cook, her boeuf bourguignon galettes
and carrot cupcakes are well worth a cycle ride to this weekly market.

SEAFOOD PAELLA £5.00

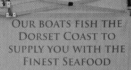

OUR BOATS FISH THE
DORSET COAST TO
SUPPLY YOU WITH THE
FINEST SEAFOOD

STEVE HALL 07785 571023
MATTHEW BALDWIN 07968 176485

UNIT 14 MARITIME BUSINES
MERESIDE, PORTLAND, D

email· Hpshellfis

TEVE

EN FROM,

VE BEEN
T WET FISH,
FISH.
M OUR

OKING
EED YOUR
ED ETC.

N BE

RDS

SEAFOOD
PAELLA £5
···
CHILLI CRAB
NOODLES £5

LOOKING FOR 3HOURS
WORK ON A TUESDAY!
PLEASE ASK!

Imperial College Farmers' Market / Hand-Picked Shellfish Co.

Queen's Lawn, Imperial College London, Exhibition Road, SW7 5NH
☎ London Farmers' Markets 020 7833 0338
Hand-Picked Shellfish Co. Steve Hall 07785 571 023, Matthew Baldwin 07968 176 485
www.lfm.org.uk/markets/south-kensington-tuesday
Open Tuesday 10am–2pm, closed Christmas Day, Boxing Day and New Year's Day
Tube Knightsbridge, South Kensington **Bus** 9, 10, 49, 52, 74, 360, 452
The market is wheelchair accessible

One of the most enticing stalls here on a Tuesday morning is the Hand-Picked Shellfish Company. Based in Dorset, two enterprising fishermen get up at 5am to catch their fish and then arrive in London a few hours later, paella dishes at the ready. Their sweet chilli crab noodles are warming and spicy, while their traditional Spanish seafood paella is perfect for a delicious, filling hot lunch. Fresh fish can also be pre-ordered in advance – from speckled lobsters to smoked mackerel or whatever they catch off the coast of Weymouth. There is also a wide variety of other produce for sale at this weekly outdoor market, from organic vegetables to venison and smoked garlic.

Bermondsey Farmers' Market

Bermondsey Square, SE1 3UN
☎ Perry Court Farm 01233 812 302, Scarlet Rosita 07923 109 170
www.perrycourtfarm.co.uk, www.scarletrositafood.co.uk
Open Saturday 10am–2pm, closed Bank Holidays
Tube Borough **Bus** 1, 42, 88, 188, C10
The market has wheelchair access and there is an adapted toilet in the cinema café opposite

Perry Court Farm is one of the largest stalls in this small South London farmers' market. As well as a wide variety of fruit and vegetables, this Kentish farm has recently started selling their own air-dried apple crisps, which are a great snack to keep you going when walking round farmers' markets. Their unsprayed seasonal fruit and vegetables include greengages, yellow sweetcorn, purple cauliflowers and cavolo nero, the long dark cabbage leaves so beloved of Italian chefs. Their produce is very cheap as there is no middleman, so visiting this market is a great way to do your weekly shop. Scarlet Rosita's raw food confectionery and baked cakes are also delicious – try their hazelnut biscotti or coffee and walnut cake.

Blackheath Farmers' Market / Seasonal Suffolk

Blackheath Station car park, SE3 9LA ☎ Seasonal Suffolk 01206 617 042
www.lfm.org.uk/markets/blackheath
Open Sunday 10am–2pm, closed Christmas Day, Boxing Day and New Year's Day
Train Blackheath **Bus** 54, 108, 202, 321, 386, B16
The market is wheelchair accessible

This lively market may not be in the prettiest location in London, but it has a wide
range of stalls, with up to 55 setting out their wares each Sunday morning. Try the
unusual pâtés and terrines produced by Seasonal Suffolk, made from mushrooms
and berries collected from East Anglian woods and fields. The owner has been
foraging for over a decade, and now shares his edible finds with London gourmets.
This is probably the only place in the capital where you can buy giant puffballs, wild
damsons, windfall crab-apples, home-smoked pigeons and pork and pistachio
terrine. The stall holder worked as a chef in Paris and his smoked and pickled
samphire, hawthorn jelly, beef and Guinness pâté and Moroccan lamb tagine
are unusual treats for a Sunday tea.

Horniman Farmers' Market

Horniman Museum Gardens, 100 London Road, Forest Hill SE23 3PQ
☎ Horniman Museum 020 8699 1872
www.horniman.ac.uk/visit/events/horniman-farmers-market
Open Saturday 9am–1.30pm
Train Forest Hill **Bus** 176, 185, 197, 365, P4
The market is wheelchair accessible and has adapted toilets inside the museum

This weekly market has the most spectacular views of any in London. With panoramic vistas over South London, this is a stunning place to find English fruit, baked goods, artisan breads, meats and other produce. Every week Brambletye Fruit Farm bring boxes of their seasonal fruit and vegetables, including rainbow chard, rocket, basil and sunshine apples to these magnificent gardens. There are also numerous stalls selling Fair Trade juice, handmade chocolates, fresh fish, scallops and different kinds of sausage rolls. The surrounding gardens are an ideal spot for an impromptu picnic, and if you buy your bread, cheese and tomatoes in the outdoor market, you won't have to carry your lunch very far.

London Bridge Farmers' Market (Guy's)

King's College London, Guy's Campus, SE1 1UL, access from Newcomen Street and St Thomas Street ☎ London Farmers' Markets 020 7833 0338
www.facebook.com/londonbridgefarmersmarket
Open Tuesday 9am–2pm **Tube** London Bridge, Borough **Bus** 17, 21, 35, 40, 43, 48, 133, 141, 149, 343, 381, 521, C10
The market is wheelchair accessible from Newcomen Street

This large farmers' market has a mixture of stalls – from those selling hot pasta and paella to tables piled high with orchard plums, delicate oyster mushrooms and bottles of freshly pressed apple juice. The fruit and vegetable stalls sell seasonal produce, so unlike the predictable supermarkets the food sold here will be surprising and different every time you visit. Bring a large basket if you are easily seduced by plump tomatoes, ruby beetroots, stiff white leeks and loaves from Aston's Bakery. Walking under the tall plane trees in Memorial Arch Square, this is one of the prettiest locations in London to do your grocery shopping.

Pimlico Farmers' Market / Wild Country Organics

Orange Square, corner of Pimlico Road and Ebury Street, SW1W 8UT
☎ London Farmers' Markets 020 7833 0338, Wild Country Organics 01223 894 599
www.lfm.org.uk/markets/pimlico-road, www.wildco.co.uk
Open Saturday 9am–1pm, closed Christmas Day, Boxing Day and New Year's Day,
open Easter Saturday
Tube Victoria **Bus** 11, 170, 211
The market is wheelchair accessible

Shopping in this small farmers' market in the middle of a leafy Pimlico square is a
really pleasant experience. Wild Country Organics' tiny round courgettes, vivid orange
squash, firm aubergines and crimson tomatoes are almost too beautiful to cook with.
As well as growing their own sorrel, pak choi and mustard greens, they even print
labels telling you the mineral and vitamin content of the vegetables. The stallholders
are invariably friendly and helpful, and the produce is more reasonably priced than
in the shops surrounding the square. Just behind the small statue of Mozart you can
also buy bunches of seasonal flowers and their shaggy, meadow-like appearance will
enhance any London kitchen table.

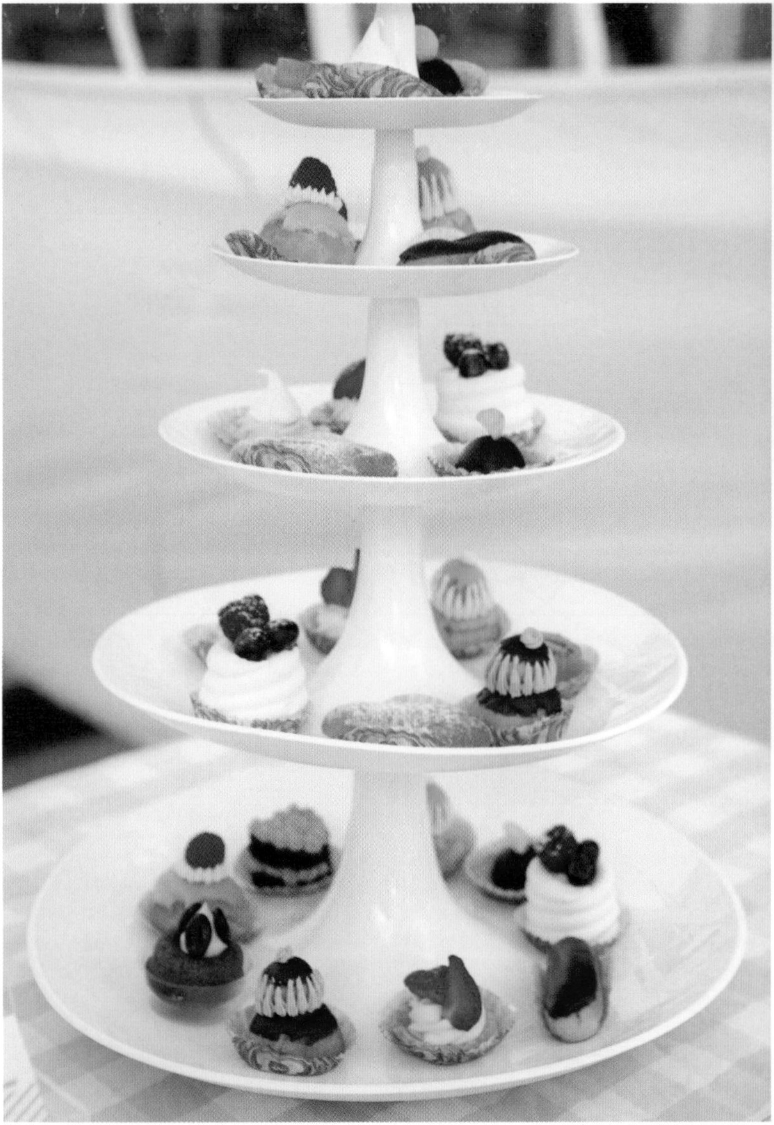

Kew Village Market / Love By Cake

Kew Station Parade, Richmond TW9 3PZ ☎ Love By Cake 020 8123 3194
www.kewvillagemarket.org
Open first Sunday of the month 10am–2pm
Tube and **Train** Kew Gardens **Bus** 65, 190, 391, 419, R68
The market is wheelchair accessible

This lively market is a treat for anyone who appreciates buying gourmet food in an informal, relaxed atmosphere. Around 35 stalls appear once a month just outside Kew Gardens station offering tasty Ethiopian dishes, bowls of black and green salted olives, bottles of real ale, French crêpes and seasonal fruit and vegetables. The Maids of Honour pie stall is a local favourite, as is the enterprising Love By Cake. This young couple bake tiny meringues, rum babas, profiteroles and other sweet delicacies. Fill a pink gingham box with a selection of their hand-made petit fours for a rather special Sunday tea.

Index